Seething Cauldron

Essays on Zoroastrianism, Sufism, Freemasonry, Wicca, Druidry, and Thelema.

Seething Cauldron: Essays on Zoroastrianism, Sufism, Freemasonry, Wicca, Druidry, and Thelema.

Copyright © 2010, Payam Nabarz

ISBN: 978-0-9556858-4-2

Includes bibliographical references and Index

Published in 2010 by 'Web of Wyrd Press'

An imprint of BECS Ltd.

http://www.webofwyrdpress.com

For mailing list: http://www.myspace.com/webofwyrdpress

All rights reserved. No part of this book may be reproduced or utilised in any form or by any means, electronic or mechanical, including photocopying, recording, or by any information storage and retrieval system, without permission in writing from the publisher.

Disclaimer: This book is intended as an informational guide only. Due caution should be taken by the reader should they decide to use any of the substances mentioned in some of the chapters herein. The author and publisher cannot take responsibility for any allergic reaction or any other negative results.

Author Biography:

Persian born Payam Nabarz is a Sufi and a practicing Dervish. He is a Druid in the *Order of Bards, Ovates and Druids*, and a co-founder of its *Nemeton of the Stars'* Grove. He is a modern day Persian Magi, a revivalist of the Temple of Mithras, and recently a Hierophant in the *Fellowship of Isis*. He has also worked with the Golden Dawn system, Thelema, Nath Tantra, Wicca, and the Craft. He is 37 and lives in England.

He was the founder *of Spirit of Peace*, a charitable organisation dedicated to personal inner peace and world peace via interfaith dialogue between different spiritual paths.

Payam Nabarz is author of *'The Mysteries of Mithras: The Pagan Belief That Shaped the Christian World'* (Inner Traditions, 2005), *'The Persian Mar Nameh: The Zoroastrian Book of the Snake Omens & Calendar'* (Twin Serpents, 2006), and *Divine Comedy of Neophyte Corax and Goddess Morrigan* (Web of Wyrd, 2008). He is also editor of *Mithras Reader An Academic and Religious Journal of Greek, Roman, and Persian Studies. Volume 1(2006), Volume 2 (2008), Volume 3 (2010),* and is author of *Stellar Magic: a Practical Guide to Rites of the Moon, Planets, Stars and Constellations* (Avalonia, 2009).

For further info visit:

www.stellarmagic.co.uk and http://www.myspace.com/nabarz

Acknowledgements

To Alison Jones for reading this manuscript and her helpful comments.

To Chesca Potter for cover art the 'Green Man'.

Each essay contains its own acknowledgment section.

> *"The wind is free, but the sand goes where it is blown; unaware of the world around it, whirling on the breath of the Gods, at the mercy of the storm that engulfs it. What is one grain of sand in the desert? One grain amongst the storm?"* –Prince of Persia VG.

> *"To see a world in a grain of sand,*
> *And a heaven in a wild flower,*
> *Hold infinity in the palm of your hand,*
> *And eternity in an hour."*
> -William Blake

Preface	7
The Persian Fool & Trickster: *Haji Firouz*	14
Anahita: Lady of Persia	23
Zoroastrian Angels and Demons	41
Mithras and the right handed handshake of the Gods	63
Influences of Freemasonry and Sufism on Wicca and Neo-Paganism	77
Introduction	77
Hermetic Order of the Golden Dawn	79
A Rough Guide to Wicca's Herstory	86
The Sufi and Theosophical Influence	94
Traditional Witchcraft and Wicca	103
Freemasonry in Wicca	107
The Craft	108
The Working Tools	108
The Charge	108
The five points of Fellowship	110
So Mote it Be	112
Merry Meet, Merry Part, Merry Meet Again	112
The Challenge	113
Properly Prepared	114
Circumambulation	116
Cowan	117
The Three Degrees	118
Initiation: First Degree	119
Initiation: Second Degree	125
Initiation: Third Degree	128
Quasi Freemasonry in Wicca	131
Conclusions	137

Sacred Plants (Drugs in religion)   **141**

   Datura and Brugsmansie   *144*

   Ololiqui and Teonanacatl   *146*

   Ayahuasca   *147*

   Homa or Soma   *149*

The Right Hand Path or Left Hand Path; Star Wars, Excalibur & Lord of the Rings.   **157**

   LHP and RHP revisited   *165*

To Genes, Memes, Gods and beyond (Sex, Chocolate & Religion).   **170**

Spirit of Peace   **186**

   Spirit of Peace - background and history   *188*

   Spirit of Peace conference I: 'Light, Life, Love, Liberty'   *193*

   Spirit of Peace conference II: 'A Day of Sacred Music and Art', in aid of Amnesty International   *199*

   Spirit of Peace conference III: 'The Nameless Path' , in the aid of 'Adopt a Minefield' project   *204*

   Spirit of Peace conference IV: The interface between mysticism-Religion-Magic, in the aid of 'Adopt a Minefield' project   *209*

   Epilogue: A blessing to peaceful demonstrators   *217*

Index   **222**

Preface

The Sufi ritual meal ceremony of the 'Deeg Jush'[1] translates as the 'Seething Cauldron' or 'Boiling Cauldron', and, like its Celtic equivalent; the Cauldron of Cerridwen, it symbolizes the transformation and change of the initiate as he/she becomes cooked in the cauldron. The 'Green Man' painting here, by Chesca Potter (the cover artwork) shows the initiate being placed in the cauldron, and then emerging as the Green Man or Khider in Sufism. The process of metamorphosis in the vat as Sufi poet and Pir Dr. Nurbakhsh describes it is:

> 'Like grapes, we have always accompanied the vat.
>
> From the view of the world, we have disappeared.
>
> For years, we boiled from the fire of love
>
> Until we became that wine which intoxicated the world.'

Seething is also a Nordic tradition technique [2] for making a connection to the Dragon energy. The title of book intends to signify the similarity of the Nordic tradition, Druidy, Sufism and a number of other magical traditions with their common motif of the boiling/ seething transformation of the seeker. Here, materials

---

[1] For further info on 'Deeg Jush' see: 'In the Paradise of the Sufis' or its recent revised edition 'The Path, Sufi practices' by Dr. Javad Nurbakhsh (Khaniqahi-Nimatullahi Publications, 2002).

[2] For further info on 'Seething' see: 'Seidways: shaking, swaying and serpent mysteries' by Jan Fries, (Mandrake, 1996).

from number of traditions are placed into one boiling pot, emphasising that each person needs to make their own journey. This collection of essays reflects my own journey and studies on the path. The majority of these essays were published in various esoteric magazines over the years for example: Touchstone (the Journal of Order of Bards, Ovates, Druids), Pagan Dawn (the Journal of the Pagan Federation), Stone Circle, The Little Red Book, Pentacle, White Dragon, Silver Star, Cauldron, Fezana (Zoroastrian Journal), and the Sufi Magazine. However, I felt it would useful to have them all collected in one volume together here.

To help explain the Deeg Jush (Seething Cauldron) ceremony and put it into context, here is a poem I wrote about it after the 2004 ceremony and event.

Deeg Jush (Seething Cauldron, at Summer Solstice 20th June 2004).

At Summer Solstice, the longest day,

The symbolic height of power of Nur[3].

Under the eye of Mithra:[4] the Sun,

In the Old Windmill[5], the Pir is turning the Millstone,

---

[3] Light.

[4] Mithra or Mehr, means Love, Sun, Friend, and kindness.

[5] The actual name of the residence of the Sufi Pir in Sulgrave, England.

metamorphosing the soul-grain of the Sufis into

bread and 'Cakes of Light'[6] to nourish all mankind.

We little raindrops, rush forth,

like the Welsh Bard Taliesin,

into the Deeg Jush -

the cauldron of transformation

to be boiled and changed.

In the 'Jam Khaneh' —the Gathering House,

All have gathered, seen and unseen,

from Earth to the Seven Heavens.

All religious and their gods across

time and space stand

shoulder to shoulder in the `Jam Khaneh'.

A Shiva statute next to a Golden Buddha,

Christ next to Allah,

next to the Horned Deer

of our cave dwelling ancestors.

---

[6] Cake of Light is the name of the eucharistic host found within Thelema.

People too have gathered from all corners

of this blue tear in space we call home.

Young and old, man and woman,

from different races and cultures and

continents: Asia, Africa, Europe,

the Americas, Australia,

all have gathered in

the `Jam Khaneh'.

Words of the Pir echoes: '5000 year old

Indo-Iranian-European (Aryan) creed of Divine Unity,

Love and Chivalry spread across

the Old World by the Aryan people'.

The outer label might have altered

through the millennia, Dervish, Sufi, Magi,

Duir, Druid, Brahmin, ... but its heart

has changed little in those

in the 'Land of the Aryans':

Iran to Eire (Ireland).

The lit torch is kept alive by many now,

and has gone beyond the land of

the Aryans, bringing light into many dark places.

In the 'Jam Khaneh', we,

like little points of light,

form a galaxy, all circling the

Qutub (pole) during Zeker –

the remembrance.

Outside of this Temple of Love,

saplings planted by us in rich soil of Oxon

many moons ago, are now tall groves

towering above our heads.

In the Oak groves, the doorway tree

of Duir opens a gateway to Otherworld.

Silver Birch tree, shimmering Lady of the Woods,

dances and moves her slender white arms

to the sound of the Tonbak -drum.

The smell of roses is intoxicating all,

in this Golestan of Love.

In the fruitful Apple Orchards,

the meaning of Avalon: Isle of Apples (Britain)

becomes clear.

The trees, the flowers, even the farmer's cows

and the bees are joining the song and dance of Unity.

Hu, Hu, Hu.

All is One and One is All.

Remember: Unity, Love, Chivalry

Haq, Haq, Haq.

'Everything' is turning, whirling

around the Qutub during ecstasy of Sama.

An eternity caught in a moment.

Hu, Hu, Hu.

Figure 1: Lord Shiva. Painting by unknown artist.

The Persian Fool & Trickster: *Haji Firouz*

This was written in around 1999 and was first published in the Sufi Magazine.

'Nothing ever becomes real till it is experienced - even a proverb is no proverb to you till your life has illustrated it.' –Keats

'Die Before You Die' -Sufi proverb

It's Nou Roz, the Spring Equinox; balance of light and darkness and the beginning of the Iranian New Year. One of the many customs for this time of year is that families visit each other and pay their respects; the 'Eid Didany'. Another custom of this festival is that of the 'Haji Firoz'; 'Haji Firoz' is a Persian comical folk figure, who dresses up similarly to English Morris (Moorish) dancers. Both Morris Dancers and Haji Firoz dress in white and bright coloured clothes and paint their faces black, ring bells, play music and bring the joy of the spring to the public, as Fools and trickster figure.

There is a difference this New Year. I am sitting in a grove of Yew trees, the Celtic tree of remembrance and transcendence over time, the place where memories flood back, and all sense of time dissolves. I am staring into the roaring flames of the bonfire in middle of the circle, the drummers are beating a steady rhythm, Ya

Hu, Ya Hu. Slowly I begin remembering the song lines from the landscape of my life.

I am 10 and going on 'Eid Didnay' with my parents, bored and uneasy for having been dragged from one house to another and having to listen to the endless well intended comments of relatives: 'Insha Allah we will attend his wedding and his graduation'. I wonder to myself what is 'free will'? One more relative to visit, before going home. I can tolerate this, I have my 'Sang Sabor' (stone of patience) in my jacket. Last call of the day, and for the twentieth time the same well-intended comments and the squeezing of my cheeks! At least I can distract myself by looking at their settee, which has images of Greek gods dancing; how typically pretentious and middle class I think to myself. Across the hallway I catch a glimpse of a man dressed in white making his way to the kitchen. I am sitting on edge of my seat, pulling on my mother's sleeve saying, 'there is a Haji Firouz in the hallway'. I am excited now, the man enters, and he has a long gray hair a long white beard and is wearing a white robe. I rejoice loudly stating: 'Haji Firouz, Haji Firouz'. The man is smiling, my mum is trying to calm me down, and introduce our host to me. I am asking why his face is not painted black? My father is embarrassed. Our host most amused, my mother sits me down finally, and explains he is not a 'Haji Firouz' but a Dervish and a Sufi. On our way out he gives a coin to my mother, the emblem of his order, and the coin has the image of Imam *'Ali'* on it.

I blink, and I am 15 and have completed all the grades in a school of Yoga, my studies of the occult are taking me to Kabbalah and ritual Magick. Library after library, hundreds of books read, fasting, vows of silence, banishing rites and purification. It's the end of October, the night of Halloween, when the veil between the worlds is said to be thin. I have sneaked into the garden, all robed up with staff and sword in hand, Seals of Solomon drawn on parchment. Feeling rather silly about the whole thing, so I giggle to myself, looking up and smile at the moon, our Lady of the crossroads. I begin the invocation: *'advoco angelos sanctos terr...'* there is a hedgehog in the grass making its way across, I completely lose the thread, all the Latin I memorized escapes my mind. The hedgehog had ended my rite. The hedgehog wasn't bothered by me, but I was bothered by her presence. I began observing nature, trees, animals and the stars, the path becoming visible.

Another blink and I am wandering through East London aged 20, dawn comes, I am spiralling down. The abyss opening, going down Bethnal Green tube station escalator, faces melt away. I am in the underworld. A train arrives and I enter, the Great Serpent swallows me. The Serpent twists and turns as it makes its way in the underworld. My body begins shutting down; I am spitting yellow venom. Time passes. My body heals but my soul still seeks union. A few weeks later I am sitting in front of a Sufi Sheik in Queens-Way, and become initiated into the Path, practicing the remembering: the 'Zeker'.

I am walking the land of England as a wandering dervish, listening to the story of the Land; Dragon lines and ancient places. The rolling mist at Chanctonbury Ring in Sussex, the Cornish coasts, waterfalls and rivers. Walking alone still, time to be with others. I set forth and create a magical space, soon we are many, travellers on the path, all sharing a nature based vision of life. We sang our songs, performed ceremonies to mark the passage of the seasons. One night around the Imbolc bonfire in February, inside a tepee, someone is playing an Irish jig on a fiddle, songs, accompanied by few drums. A shaman among us starts chanting a Native American chant, moments later I am chanting the Sufi chant *Hagan Hagan Ya Hagan'* (Truth). The chants, the songs and the music from all over the world fuse together. The divine beauty from all corners of this single blue tear in space we call earth unite, we are all seeing the same elephant in the room.

It is summer solstice, we have spent the night singing within the Avebury stone circle as previous years. Dawn arrives, marking the end of the night vigil, the carnival atmosphere is peaking, even the police are smiling, and perhaps they are saying thanks for not being stationed at the front line of Stonehenge. Fire jugglers, spiral dancers, drummers and peaceful Druids, hippies, Thelemites, we all are celebrating. I wander off to a quiet spot, sun rises and somehow

I am performing the 'Namarz' and chanting *'Ya dost Mithra'* (the trinity of Sun, Love, Friend). I overhear a cheerful song. A group of priestess are singing the 'Charge of the Goddess': *'If you do not find what you seek within thee, you shall not find it without thee, behold I have been with thee from the beginning; and I am that which is attained in the end.'* I see a crow feasting on the remains of my breakfast, she seems content and happy, so I ask the crow: 'have you seen the bird Simurgh? Well if you do, let her know we are looking for her!'

Time is passing and I am walking the land still, it's the Ridgeway, the oldest trackway in England. At Wayland's Smithy an ancient long barrow, the gates of dreaming open, pointing to Italy. Rationality disappears and I catch the next flight to Italy; I travel to Ostia, south of Rome. The river carries me, no idea where. I am heading west in search of enlightenment, while everyone else is heading east, I guess the grass is always greener on the other side! There are remains of Temples of Mithras, the Persian solar god of truth and justice in England, dated to 400AD. All of my streams meet within me, and are no longer at conflict.

Blink, Blink, I am heading towards Glastonbury, its another 'Nou Roz'. The comet 'Hale Bopp' dominates the night sky, flanking it are the constellations Orion and the Plough, symbols of the Egyptians gods Horus and Seth: order and chaos as always opposing each other. My expectations are running high, Glastonbury, a pilgrim centre for centuries, where the body of King

Arthur lies, a place filled with mystery? I am excited! Whom will I meet? Druids, Wiccans or magicians, musicians or New Age travellers? So many exciting and colourful characters I could meet, by the Glastonbury Tor. After days of walking, the Tor is in sight. I rush up the hill with a full backpack, breathing heavily and completely exhausted from the journey. A couple of people are playing the 'didgeridoo'. I can hear people talking about Kabbalah. I am in the right place; here is knowledge! Sadly a middle aged man, in a gray jacket who is not looking at all like a hippie, strikes a conversation with me. I am annoyed; he looks boring and not even a long hair or a beard. I try to ignore him, concentrating on the 'didgeridoo' players, who look much more interesting, and fitted my expectations. Eventually I begin talking to him out of politeness, about the weather of course. He introduces himself, his name is Ali and he is Sufi. Feels like a bucket of water has fallen on my head, I began laughing and laughing at my own foolishness. Remembering the Sufi proverb: *'Where I run to, it's your face I see'*.

I stayed in Glastonbury for a few days, and when I wasn't laughing at myself, I was in Zeker. Before leaving, I visited the Tor once more at sunset, carrying out Zeker silently. A young drunk was disturbing everyone, and most people left. The sunset was beautiful and as time passed, the Zeker was all that was 'Hu.. Hu..'. I feel a pressure on my throat and slowly open my eyes; the young drunken lad is pressing a large blade to my throat. I am not disturbed by his presence; 'Hu Hu' is still vibrating in me. There is only love. I hear my voice tell him to remove the knife and go. I only feel love for him, Jesus' word ringing in my head: ' Forgive them Father, as they know not what they do'. He moves away quietly. Hu… Hu...

Blink, blink, time passes. The Labour Party finally comes into power (1997), Iran beats USA 2-1 at football (1998 World Cup), the Human Genome Project is complete, and the World Wide Web expands rapidly. For me studies into Wicca, Druidry, Thelema, Shamanism all flow, threads being woven fast, complete madness follows. *'Divaneh sho, divaneh sho, mastaneh sho, mastaneh sho'* (Become mad, become mad, become drunk become drunk). I am attending a Sufi 'Deeg-Jush' gathering in Queens-Way, London. The word *'Deeg-Jush'* translates as 'boiling or seething cauldron', and, like its Celtic equivalent, the Cauldron of Cerridwen, it symbolises the transformation and change of the initiate as he/she becomes cooked in the cauldron. Hu… Hu... I am tired from the day's work and fall asleep during the proceedings. I dream: I am floating in outer space, among the stars, I think to myself perhaps I've been watching too much *'Star Trek'*! But then suddenly an intense sense of fear engulfs me, and my awareness of the others in the room changes. Am I asleep or awake? Consensus reality seems to have left the building! I am out in space in front of a gigantic spider's web, the web stretches for thousands of miles in all directions, and Arachne sits in the middle. My instinct is to fly away, to run away again. The fear of being eaten by the spider, but no more running away, I fly towards the web. I am flying faster and faster towards it and then let myself get wrapped in the web, the silvery threads wrap around me, choking me. My heart is beating fast *'Mola Hagan Hagan Hagan'* (centre of Truth), the black spider then begins eating me, biting my body and tearing me; the Shamanic dismemberment. The pain and fear is intense, I am boiling and screaming, the 'I' is in agony. As the spider eats me, I slowly became part of her. I feel myself slowly growing inside her. Embryo to infant, to child in a moment. I began rising within her body, she is giving birth to me! As I emerge, my body appears to be made of golden light rather than of flesh. The spider begins turning golden in her colour too, the spider is becoming part of me: we become one. I am standing as a man glowing golden like a star in middle of the web several hundred feet tall among all the other stars in space. The colour of the web begins turning to gold, finally a golden web of light is running throughout space, everything in the universe is connected, and all is one: every man and woman is a Star. I hear a voice saying *'Ya Hag'*; it's the voice of the Bestower of Light (Nurbakhsh) marking the end of the 'Deeg Jush' gathering. I wake up from my dream, and perhaps enter another. As I open my eyes, for a moment I am aware of golden rays connecting everyone in the room together. Each person is a Sun at the centre of his or her own web of light, yet all connected: Unity.

It's Nou Roz, deep in the forest our bonfire is still burning. Drums are still beating. I am 27, being the bird Simurgh, remembering the Old ones: In the west 'Anahita', goddess of the seas. In the north 'Zamin', the earth. In the east, 'Vau' lord of air, in the south 'Atar' fiery son of Ahura Mazda. All around is the Green Cloaked one, Khider; the Friend of Sufis. We are dancing with the fire, remembering in our own ways. I am slowly melting, from far away I hear my own voice chanting 'Hu, Hu'. From afar an Owl joins in the chorus 'Huoo Huoo'. Feeling the cycle of seasons pass one by one rapidly, leaves falling, buds opening, the fire of life running in the veins of the Land. I am remembering all of time, all of life in a moment, I am ten again, laughing with the 'Haji Firoz' during the 'Eid Didany'.

Anahita: Lady of Persia

The following is based on the Anahita chapter from *The Mysteries of Mithras: The Pagan Belief That Shaped the Christian World*, by Payam Nabarz, Inner Traditions, 2005. It appeared in *From a Drop of Water*, Avalonia 2009 in this much extended format.

Mighty Anahita with splendour will shine,

Incarnated as a youthful divine.

Full of charm her beauty she will display,

Her hip with charming belt she will array.

Straight-figured, she is as noble bride,

Freeborn, herself in puckered dress will hide.

Her cloak is all decorated with gold,

With precious dress Anahita we shall behold.

-(Original poem based on Kashani's Persian folk songs, from an Avestan invocation to Anahita)

Dusk of Shabe Yalda (Yule) 777 BCE, somewhere on a beach by the Caspian sea. A young Magi (who may later known as the prophet Zoroaster) has been keeping a night vigil. His solitary fire is the only light for miles around and his recitation of Aban

Yasht - the hymn to angel-goddess Anahita - the only sound to be heard apart from the waves gently crashing onto the beach:

'Angel-Goddess of all the waters upon the earth and the source of the cosmic ocean; she who drives a chariot pulled by four horses: wind, rain, cloud, and sleet; your symbol is the eight-rayed star. You are the source of life, purifying the seed of all males and the wombs of all females, also cleansing the milk in the breasts of all mothers. Your connection with life means warriors in battle prayed to you for survival and victory.

A maid, fair of body, most strong, tall-formed, high-girded, pure, . . . wearing a mantle fully embroidered with gold; ever holding the haresma [sacred plant] in your hand, . . . you wear square golden earrings on your ears . . . a golden necklace around your beautiful neck, . . . Upon your head . . . a golden crown, with a hundred stars, with eight rays . . . with fillets streaming down.'[7]

The Magi's prayer is answered by the sea in the form of a vision; as midnight approaches and time slows, the sea parts. A large silver throne appears; on either side of it sits a lion with eyes of blue flame. On the throne sits a Lady in silver and gold garments, proud and tall, an awe-inspiring warrior-woman, as terrifying as she is beautiful. Tall and statuesque she sits, her noble origins evident in her appearance, her haughty authority made clear and commanding through a pair of flashing eyes. A dove flies above her and a peacock walks before her. A crown of shining gold rings her royal temples; bejeweled with eight sunrays and one hundred stars, it

---

[7] From verses 126–128 of the Aban Yasht 5.

holds her lustrous hair back from her beautiful face. Her marble-like white arms reflect moonlight and glisten with moisture. She is clothed with a garment made of thirty beaver skins, and it shines with the full sheen of silver and gold. The planet Venus shines brightly in the sky.[8]

Time passes... history takes place...

---

[8] This description of Anahita is based on her description in Tony Allan, Charles Phillips, and Michael Kerrigan, Myth and Mankind series: *Wise Lord of the Sky: Persian Myth* (London: Time Life Books, 1999), 32.

Figure 2: Goddess Anahita, painting by Akashnath, 2008.

Circa 400 BCE Achaemenian king Artaxerxes II Mnemon (404-359 BCE) inscribes in Ecbatana in his palace:

'*Artaxerxes, the great king, the king of kings, the king of all nations, the king of this world, the son of king Darius [II Nothus], Darius the son of king*

Artaxerxes [I Makrocheir], Artaxerxes the son of king Xerxes, Xerxes the son of king Darius, Darius the son of Hystaspes, the Achaemenid, says: this hall [apadana] I built, by the grace of Ahuramazda, Anahita, and Mithra. May Ahuramazda, Anahita, and Mithra protect me against evil, and may they never destroy nor damage what I have built.' [9]

Artaxerxes II, like other Achaemenian kings, was initiated by priests at a sanctuary of Anahita in Pasargadai during his coronation. Artaxerxes II built the temple of Anahita at Kangavar near Kermanshah as well as many others. The Kangavar was a magnificent temple four-fifths of a mile in circumference, built using cedar or cypress trees. All the columns and floor-tiles were covered with gold and silver. It was perhaps one of the most breathtaking buildings ever built in the Middle East.

Anahita's role as the goddess of water, rain, abundance, blessing, fertility, marriage, love, motherhood, birth, and victory became well established. This goddess was the manifestation of women's perfection. Ancient kings were crowned by their queens in Anahita's temple in order to gain her protection and support. Anahita's blessing would bring fertility and abundance to the country. [10]

---

[9] See: http://www.livius.org/aa-ac/achaemenians/A2Ha.html

[10] Official entry on Anahita by the Embassy of the Islamic Republic of Iran in Ottawa, Canada on their Web site:
http://www.salamiran.org/Women/General/Women_And_Mythical_Deities.html

Time passes... history takes place... The Achaemenid Empire falls to 'Alexander the Accursed' in 330 BCE...

Circa 200 BCE sees the dedication of a Seleucid temple in western Iran to *'Anahita, the Immaculate Virgin Mother of the Lord Mithra'*.[11] The blend of Greek and Persian cultures manifest themselves in the Seleucid dynasty.

Time passes... history takes place...

The Parthian Empire (circa 247 BCE-226 CE) replaces the Seleucid and the Parthians expand the Anahita temple at Kangavar.

---

[11] First Iranian Goddess of productivity and values by Manouchehr Saadat Noury - Persian Journal, Jul 21, 2005.
http://www.iranian.ws/iran_news/publish/printer_8378.shtml

Figure 3: Bronze head of the goddess Anahita, Hellenistic Greek, 1st century BCE found at the ancient city of Satala, modern Sadak, north-eastern Turkey, now in The British Museum.

Time passes... history takes place...

Mark Anthony marches in to Armenia (circa 37 BCE - 34 BCE), and in one of the latter campaigns reached the Anahita temple at Erez:

The temple of Erez was the wealthiest and the noblest in Armenia, according to Plutarch. During the expedition of Mark Antony in Armenia, the statue was broken to pieces by the Roman soldiers. Pliny the Elder gives us the

29

following story about it: The Emperor Augustus, being invited to dinner by one of his generals, asked him if it were true that the wreckers of Anahit's statue had been punished by the wrathful goddess. 'No, answered the general, on the contrary, I have today the good fortune of treating you with one part of the hip of that gold statue.' The Armenians erected a new golden statue of Anahit in Erez, which was worshiped before the time of St. Gregory the Illuminator.' [12]

Time passes... history takes place...

The Sassanian Empire is formed ca. 226 CE. The Temple of Anahita in Bishapur was built during the Sassanian era (241-635 CE). The temple is believed to have been built by some of the estimated seventy thousand Roman soldiers and engineers who were captured by the Persian King Shapur (241-272 CE), who also captured three Roman emperors: Gordian III, Phillip, and Valerian. The design of the temple is noteworthy: water from the river Shapur is channeled into an underground canal to the temple and flows under and all around the temple, giving the impression of an island. The fire altar would have been in the middle of the temple, with the water flowing underground all around it. One might interpret this as a union of water—Anahita—with fire—Mithra.[13]

---

[12] A History of Armenia By Vahan M. Kurkjian, Bakuran. IndoEuropeanPublishing.com, 2008.

[13] For the Temple of Anahita at Bishapur, see http://www.vohuman.org/SlideShow/Anahita%20Bishapur/AnahitaBishapur00.htm

Figure 4: The Temple of Anahita in Bishapur, Iran, (Photograph by Jamshid Varza, www.vohuman.org, reproduced with his kind permission).

The Temple of Anahita in Bishapur, Iran, on the site of the ancient city built by Shapur I, Sassanian Emperor (241 C.E.–272 CE) in celebration of his victory over three Roman Emperors - Gordian III, Phillip, and Valerian.

Time passes... history takes place...

The Sassanian Empires fades and Islam arrives in Iran 637CE.

By 900 CE, Moslem pilgrims make their way to the 1100 year-old shrine of Bibi Shahr Banoo, the Islamic female saint, near the old town of Rey (South of Tehran). The town of Rey is thought to be 5000 years old, and the site of this shrine with its waterfall is believed by some to have once been an Anahita shrine. It is also close to the Cheshmeh Ali Hill (the spring of Ali Hill), which is dated to 5000 years ago. Perhaps this is an echo of Mithra-Anahita shrines being located close to each other and then becoming linked to later Islamic saints, a process seen frequently in Christianized Europe too; for example, sites sacred to the Celtic goddess Brighid became sites dedicated to Saint Brigit.

Furthermore, according to Susan Gaviri: *Anahita in Iranian Mythology* (1993):

'*...it must not be forgotten that many of the famous fire temples in Iran were, in the beginning, Anahita temples. Examples of these fire temples are seen in some* *parts of Iran, especially in Yazad, where we find that after the Muslim victory these were converted to Mosques.*'[14]

Time passes... history takes place...

Pilgrims continue to visit the Pre-Islamic Zoroastrian shrine of Pir e Sabz, or Chek Chek ('drip drip,' the sound of water dripping), in the mountains of Yazd. This is still a functional temple and the holiest site for present-day Zoroastrians living in Iran, who take their annual pilgrimage to Pir e Sabz Banu, 'the old woman in the mountain,' also called Pir e Sabz, 'the green saint,' at the beginning of summer. *Pir* means "elder," and it can also mean "fire." The title of Pir also connotes a Sufi master. *Sabz* means green.[15]

Pilgrims also continue to visit Pir e Banoo Pars (Elder Lady of Persia) and Pir e Naraki located near Yazd. The Pir Banoo temple is in an area that has a number of valleys; the name of the place is Hapt Ador, which means Seven Fires.[16]

Time passes... history takes place...

---

[14] *Anahita in Iranian Mythology*, p.7 (1993). This book is in Persian—translation here by Nabarz.

[15] For the temple at Pir-e-Sabz, see http://www.vohuman.org/SlideShow/Pir-e-Sabz/Pir-e-Sabz-1.htm

[16] For the temples of Pir e Banoo Pars and Pir e Naraki, see http://www.sacredsites.com/middle_east/iran/zoroastrian.htm

Figure 5: Commemorative gold coin with image of Anahita, 1997.

The Central Bank of Armenia in 1997, issues a commemorative gold coin with an image of Anahita on it. The bank states:

'This commemorative coin issued by the Central Bank of Armenia is devoted to Goddess Anahit. Anahit has been considered the Mother Goddess of Armenians, the sacred embodiment and patron for the crop, fruitfulness and fertility. In 34 BC, the Romans have plundered the country town Yeriza of the Yekeghiats Province in the Higher Hayk, where the huge golden statue to Anahit was situated. They smashed the statue to pieces and shared among the soldiers as pillage. On the turn of the 19th century, a head part of a bronze statue referring to Anahit was found in Satagh (Yerznka region), which is presently kept in British Museum.'[17]

Time passes... history takes place...

---

[17] http://www.cba.am/CBA_SITE/currency/aanahit.html?__locale=en

The higher social status of women in Iranian society compared to its Arab neighbours has been suggested by some to be due to its long respect for Lady Anahita. Indeed, the first Muslim woman to win a Noble Peace Prize (2003) was from Iran.

Time passes.... history take place..... Yet she is still remembered....

'Tomorrow (21.8.03), I (Jalil Nozari) *will take part in a ceremony to commemorate a very poor, old woman, a relative of mine, who died recently. Her name was Kaneez. The name in modern Farsi has negative connotations, meaning a "female servant." But, in Pahlavi, the language spoken in central Iran before the coming of Islam, it meant "a maiden," a virgin, unmarried girl. Indeed, it has both meanings of the English "maid." Anahita, too, means virgin, literally not defiled. But this is not the end of story. When I was a child, there was a place in Ramhormoz, my hometown, which now is under a city road. In it, there was a small, single-room building with a small drain pipe hanging from it. Women in their ninth month and close to delivery time stood under this pipe and someone poured water through it. There was the belief that getting wet under the drain would assure a safe delivery of the baby. The building was devoted to Khezer (the green one).* [18] *Yet, the cult is very old and clearly one of Anahita's. The role of water and safe child delivery are both parts of the Anahita cult. My deceased aunt, our Kaneez, was a servant of this building. The building was demolished years ago to build a road, and Kaneez is no more. I wonder how will we reconstruct those eras, so close to us in time yet so*

---

[18] There is a folk tradition about Saint Khezer or Khider (the green one): if one washes (pours water) on one's front door at dawn for forty days, he will appear. Khider is described as being a friend of the Sufis, and is said to stand at the boundary of sea and land. He is also said to have drunk from the fountain of immortality

far from our present conditions. It is also of interest that there exist remains of a castle, or better to say a fort, in Ramhormoz, that is called "Mother and Daughter." It belongs to the Sasanides era. "Daughter," signifying virginity, directs the mind toward Anahita. There are other shrines named after sacred women, mostly located beside springs of water. These all make the grounds for believing that Ramhormoz was one of the oldest places for Anahita worshippers.' [19]

Time passes....

Figure 6: Goddess Anahita Sculpture by Jenny Richards (2009); among water lilies, photo by P. Nabarz.

---

[19] Personal communication from Jalil Nozari, August 20, 2003.

Figure 7: Goddess Anahita Sculpture by Jenny Richards (2009); among water lilies, photo by P. Nabarz.

2004 CE. Another seeker (Nabarz) meditating by a sea makes an observation on relationships between Mehr and Aban (modern Persian names for Mithra and Anahita.) The Autumn Equinox marks the beginning of the Persian month of Mehr, and the start of the festival of Mehregan. The month of the sun god Mithra is followed by the month of the sea goddess Anahita (according to ancient sources both the partner and mother of Mithra). The month of the sun thus leads into the month of the sea. The sun sets into the ocean. The sunset over the ocean is one of the most beautiful sights there is; as the sun unites with the ocean, the light is reflected upon the water.

Mehr, coming together with Aban, gives rise to a third word: *mehraban*, which translates as 'kindness,' or 'one who is kind'. Thus, this metaphorical child of light that comes out of the marriage between Sun and Sea is *kindness*. The child of light is the Inner Light, which is in everyone. The Sun (light of God) and the Sea (divine ocean), united within each person, creates perhaps the most important spiritual quality - that of human kindness.

Time passes...

2777 C.E. Somewhere on a beach by the Caspian Sea. A young Magi has been keeping a night vigil. His solitary fire is the only light for miles around and his recitation of Aban Yasht, the hymn to angel-goddess Anahita, the only sound to be heard apart from the waves gently crashing onto the beach... She is remembered.

Further reading:

The Mysteries of Mithras: The Pagan Belief That Shaped the Christian World, by Payam Nabarz. Inner Traditions, 2005.

Wise Lord of the Sky: Persian Myth, by Tony Allan, Charles Phillips, and Michael Kerrigan. Myth and Mankind series. Time Life Books, 1999

Anahita in Iranian Mythology, (Anahita dar usturah ha-yi Irani), by Susan Gaviri. Tehran, Intisharat-i Jamal al Haqq, (year 1372), 1993.

First Iranian Goddess of productivity and values, by Manouchehr Saadat Noury in *the Persian Journal, Iranian.ws,* Jul 21, 2005.

The Avestan Hymn to Mithra trans. Ilya Gershevitch. Cambridge University Press, 2008.

The Heritage of Persia, by Richard N. Frye. Mazda, 1993.

Textual sources for the study of Zoroastrianism by Mary Boyce. University of Chicago Press, 1990.

Aban Yasht online translation at http://www.avesta.org/ka/yt5sbe.htm

Figure 8: Pond, photo by P. Nabarz.

Figure 9: Sea, photo by P. Nabarz

Zoroastrian Angels and Demons

This was written in 2009 and first published in *'Both side of Heaven'* anthology, by Avalonia press.

Figure 10: The Faravahar symbol in Zoroastrianism represents the Fravashi (person's Guardian Angel/spirit), they come down from heaven to stand by each person from their birth and are prayed to for guidance and protection. They are called the Bountiful Immortals

'I confess myself a worshipper of Mazda(Wise), a follower of Zarathushtra, one who hates the Daevas(demons) , and obeys the laws of Ahura (Lord); For sacrifice, prayer, propitiation, and glorification unto [Havani], the holy and master of holiness. . . .Unto Mithra, the lord of wide pastures, who has a

thousand ears, ten thousand eyes...' -from the Zoroastrian Hymn to Mithra.[20]

One of the oldest examples of the gods of one religion becoming the demons of another is perhaps seen in late Hinduism and late Zoroastrianism. This disparity can be viewed as a wave of new gods and their people battling the older gods and their worshipers. The Zoroastrian God and Angels are called Ahuras (Lords) and Zoroastrian false gods or demons are called Dev (Daevas), while in Hinduism the Gods are called Deva and demons Asuras (Ahuras). The positioning of Ahuras versus Devas is a later development in both religions, while in earlier periods they were seen as gods worshiped by different people: those of Indo-Iranian/Indo-European (Aryans) origins and the followers of the native Vedic religions of India.[21] The spread of Aryan pantheon into India and the subsequent blending of Aryan gods and Vedic gods provides the rich and diverse pantheon present in India today. In addition to Hinduism the Deva are seen in a more positive light than the Asuras in Buddhism too. However, the focus and scope of this article is the Zoroastrian form of Ahuras and Devas, rather than Hindu or Buddhist interpretations.

The Prophet Zarathustra (Greek name of Zoroaster) was a religious reformer, priest, visionary and prophet who brought about

---

[20] 'Hymn to Mithra' was translated from the Avesta by James Darmesteter and printed in Sacred Books of the East, American Edition, 1898, part of Oxford University Press's Sacred Books of the East (SBE) series.

[21] A History of Religious Ideas: Vol 1 From the Stone Age to the Eleusinian Mysteries by Mircea Eliade Collins (1978).

what could be seen as the reformation of Persian polytheism. The end product was probably the world's first monotheistic religion, long before Judaism, Christianity and Islam. There are differing views regarding whether Zoroaster even predates the Pharaoh Akhenaten and his monotheistic worship of Aten. Zoroaster formed a new religion out of the old Persian forms of worship and different tribal religions and regional sects. Over many more centuries, this religion, Zoroastrianism, slowly gained in popularity and finally became the state religion of the Persian Empire until the rise of Islam. This religion continued to be practised despite pressure and persecution by some Islamic rulers; it is still being practised today, with followers across the globe.

Zoroaster is thought to have lived in north eastern Iran sometime in the sixth or fifth century BCE, though some scholars believe it could have been as early as 1400 BCE. Zoroaster is said to have had a miraculous birth: his mother, Dughdova, was a virgin who conceived him after being visited by a shaft of light. Zoroaster's teachings led to the world's first monotheistic religion, in which Ahura Mazda, the "Wise Lord" of the sky, was the ultimate creator. In this religious reform, many gods and goddesses of the Persian pantheon were stripped of their sovereignty and their powers and attributes were bestowed upon the one god; Ahura Mazda.

The Avesta is the Zoroastrian holy book. It is a collection of holy texts, which include the Gathas (the word of the prophet Zoroaster himself) and the Yashts, the ancient liturgical poems and hymns that scholars believe predated Zoroaster and were modified to reflect the reformation. It also contains rituals, precepts for daily life and rites of passage for birth, marriage, and death. Because of the Avesta, the Zoroastrians were the first 'people of the book'. Avesta probably means *'authoritative utterance.'*[22]

The Gathas are seen as the original teaching by Prophet Zoroaster, other texts in the Avesta belong to Zoroastrian body of texts, some of which predate Zoroaster and some are later than Zoroaster himself. In some cases, like that of Zurvanism, it is refered to as an offshoot and a heresy. The scope of this article is the whole of Avesta and Zoroastrian body of texts and not limited to the Gathas. In the Gathas the concept of angels and demons are abstract figures and ideas, while in earlier texts and later texts they are substantive figures and beings.

Some of the Yashts are hymns to ancient Persian deities, who in Zoroastrianism are demoted to the ranks of archangels or angels, with Ahura Mazda at the top of the hierarchy. In the Zoroastrian religion, Ahura Mazda has seven immortal aspects - the Amshaspends or Spenta Mainyu (Ameshas Spenta), each of which rules over a particular realm. These holy heptads are: Vohu Mano (good thought, the realm of animals), Asha Vahishta (righteousness, the realm of fire), Spenta Armaiti (devotion, the realm of earth), Khshathra Vairya (dominion, the realm of air, sun and heavens),

---

[22] Peter Clark, Zoroastrianism: An Introduction to an Ancient Faith (Sussex: Academic Press, 1998), x.

Haurvatat (wholeness, the realm of water), Ameretat (immortality, the realm of plants), and Spenta Mainyu, who is identified with Ahura Mazda (the realm of humanity). There are also seven Yazatas, the protective spirits: Anahita (water / fertility), Atar (fire), Homa (the healing plant), Sraosha (obedience / hearer of prayers), Rashnu (judgment), Mithra (truth), Tishtrya (the Dog Star / source of rain).[23] These can be seen in the following diagram. This figure shows the seven Ameshas Spentas and the seven Yazatas.

---

[23] Cotterell, Arthur, The Ultimate Encyclopedia of Mythology, Hermes House, 2003.

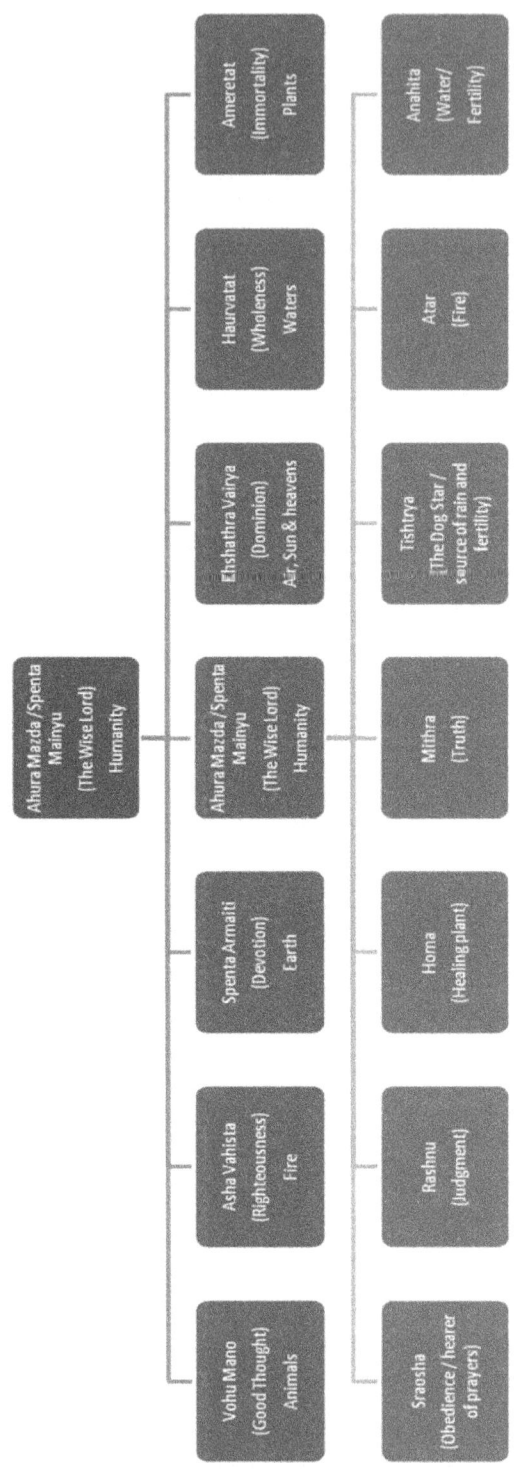

Zoroastrianism is monotheistic, with a strong sense of dualism, whereby Ahura Mazda's Ameshas Spenta and Yazatas, the forces of light and Truth (*Asha*), are faced with the forces of darkness of the Angra Mainyu, or Ahriman, who is called the Great Lie (*Druj*). He and his demons are said to create drought, harsh weather, sickness, disease, poverty, and all forms of suffering. The holy heptads the Amshaspends are faced by the unholy heptads, their polar opposites and antithesis.

Arch demons	Archangels
Angra Mainyu (main)	Spenta Mainyu (main)
Indra	Asha Vahishta
Sauru	Khshathra Vairya
Naunghaithya	Spenta Armaiti
Tauru	Haurvatat
Zairi	Ameretat
Akem-mano	Vohu-mano

There were sixteen perfect lands/countries created by Ahura Mazda and as many plagues created by Angra Mainyu to destroy them. Here are some of examples:

Plagues sent by Angra Mainyu	Main characteristic of the land or peoples created Ahura Mazda
Snakes	Rivers
Locusts	Pastures for the plants
Plundering by soldiers and thieves	Strength to the people and land allowing defence to be achieved

Ants	Corn fields
Doubt	Faith
Created tears and wailing	Mourning by leaving the house
Idolatry	Belief
The Sin of Pride	Rich pastures
Unnatural sin	(Not clear)
Burying the dead	Beauty of the landscape

Angra Mainyu creates 99,999 diseases; Ahura Mazda counters with the Holy Manthra and with the Airyaman prayer.

The Greek writer Plutarch also refers to the holy heptads:

XLVII. They too, nevertheless, tell many fabulous stories concerning their gods—for example, the following: that Oromazes (Ahura Mazda) sprang out of the purest Light, but Arimanios (Ahriman/ Angra Mainyu) out of Darkness; they wage war upon each other. Oromazes created six gods, the first of Goodwill, the second of Truth, the third of Order, of the rest one of Wisdom, one of Wealth, one of Pleasure in things beautiful. The other God created, as it were, opponents to these deities, equal in number. Then Oromazes, having augmented himself threefold, severed from the Sun as much space as the Sun is distant from Earth, and adorned the heavens with stars; and one star he appointed before all for guard and look out, namely Sirius. And having created four-and-twenty other gods, he shut them up in an egg; but those made by Arimanios, being as many as they, pierced the egg that had been laid, and so the bad things were mixed up with the good. But a time appointed by fate is coming, in which Arimanios having brought on famine and pestilence must needs be destroyed by the same and utterly vanish; when the earth becoming plain and level there shall be one life and one government of men, all happy and of one language' [24]

The battle wages across all realms, in the Zoroastrian Vendidad texts the Daevas are named:

'10.9 I drive away Indra, I drive away Sauru, I drive away the daeva Naunghaithya, from this house, from this borough, from this town, from this land; from the very body of the man defiled by the dead, from the very body of the woman defiled by the dead; from the master of the house, from the lord of the borough, from the lord of the town, from the lord of the land; from the whole of the world of Righteousness. I drive away Tauru, I drive away Zairi, from this house, from this borough, from this town, from this land; from the very body of the man defiled by the dead, from the very body of the woman defiled by the dead; from the master of the house, from the lord of the borough, from the lord of the town, from the lord of the land; from the whole of the holy world.' [25]

And furthermore:

'19.43. They cried about, their minds wavered to and fro, Angra Mainyu the deadly, the Daeva of the Daevas; Indra the Daeva, Sauru the Daeva, Naunghaithya the Daeva, Taurvi and Zairi; Aeshma of the murderous spear; Akatasha the Daeva; Winter, made by the Daevas; the deceiving, unseen Death; Zaurva, baneful to the fathers; Buiti the Daeva; Driwi the Daeva; Daiwi the Daeva; Kasvi the Daeva; Paitisha the most Daeva-like amongst the Daevas. And the evil-doing Daeva, Angra Mainyu, the deadly, said: What! let

---

[24] Plutarch's Morals: Theosophical Essays 'On Isis and Osiris; tr. by Charles William King, 1908, http://www.sacred-texts.com/cla/plu/pte/pte04.htm

[25] Vendidad http://www.avesta.org/vendidad/vd10sbe.htm

the wicked, evil-doing Daevas gather together at the head of Arezura (gate of hell)! They rush away shouting, the wicked, evil-doing Daevas; they run away shouting, the wicked, evil doing Daevas; they run away casting the Evil Eye, the wicked, evil-doing Daevas: Let us gather together at the head of Arezura! For he is just born the holy Zarathushtra, in the house of Pourushaspa. How can we procure his death? He is the weapon that fells the fiends: he is a counter-fiend to the fiends; he is a Druj to the Druj. Vanished are the Daeva worshippers, the Nasu made by the Daeva, the false-speaking Lie!They rush away shouting, the wicked, evil-doing Daevas, into the depths of the dark, raging world of hell. [26]

Other examples of binary opposites in creation are: when Ahura Mazda created the stars and constellations, Ahriman created the planets; when Ahura Mazda created the dog, Ahriman created the wolf; when Ahura Mazda created cattle and domestic animals Ahriman created animals of their opposite. Plutarch mentions a rite to Ahriman where some of his animals are listed:

'XLVI. And this is the opinion of most men, and those the wisest, for they believe, some that there are Two Gods, as it were of opposite trades—one the creator of good, the other of bad things; others call the better one "God," the other Dæmon, as did Zoroaster the Magian, who, they record, lived 5,000 years before the Trojan War. He therefore calls the former Oromazes, the latter Arimanios; and furthermore explains that of all the objects of sense, the one most resembles Light, the other Darkness, and Ignorance; and that Mithras is between the two, for which reason the Persians call Mithras the "Mediator,"

---

[26] Vendidad http://www.avesta.org/vendidad/vd19sbe.htm#section6

and he (Zoroaster) taught them to offer sacrifice of vows and thanksgiving to the one, of deprecation and mourning to the other. For they bruise a certain herb called omoine in a mortar and invoke Hades and Darkness, and mixing it with the blood of a wolf they have sacrificed, they carry away and throw it into a place where the Sun never comes, for of plants they believe some to belong to the good God, others to the evil Dæmon; and similarly of animals, dogs, birds, and land hedgehogs belong to the Good, but to the Bad One water rats, for which reason they hold happy men that have killed the greatest number of such things.' [27]

The Zoroastrian dualistic idea of Good versus Evil was inherited by Judaism and then Christianity and Islam; indeed, it is possible to trace the axis of evil-versus-good theology and mentality from Zoroaster to all the current monotheistic world religions. The Zoroastrian scholar Mary Boyce describes the Zoroastrian text about *Viraz's* vision of heaven and hell as the ultimate source of Dante's Divine Comedy.

The Zoroastrian sequence of legends of 'saviour' and 'anti-saviour' figures has many parallels with the Book of Revelations. To illustrate some of parallels:

1) The theme of the saviour (*Saoshyan*t) sent from god.

2) The antichrist (*evil sent from Ahirman*).

3) The whore of Babylon (*Jeh the whore*).

4) The last judgment (*Frashegrid*).

---

[27] Plutarch's Morals: Theosophical Essays 'On Isis and Osiris; tr. by Charles William King, 1908, http://www.sacred-texts.com/cla/plu/pte/pte04.htm

5) The end of times (*Khshathra*), and the resurrection of the dead.
6) The fiery horseman to bring the world to end.

In this Zoroastrian eternal battle of light and darkness, Mithra is the great warrior who, according to his hymn (Yasht 10), carries the hundred-knotted mace or club with a hundred edges, "the strongest of all weapons, the most victorious of all weapons, from whom Angra Mainyu, who is all death, flees away with fear." (Today, Zoroastrian priests still carry the mace of Mithra, which is given to them at their ordination as a symbol of fighting evil.) Even though the old gods were stripped of their power, Mithra had such wide popularity and importance that the Zoroastrians adapted the stories concerning him and gave him a prominent place in their religion.

The end times is referred to by Plutarch:

Theopomus (born c. 380 B.C.) says that, according to the Magians, for three thousand years alternatively the one god will dominate the other and be dominated, and that for another three thousand years they will fight and make war, until one smashes up the domain of the other. In the end Hades (Ahriman) shall perish and men shall be happy; neither shall they need sustenance nor shall they cast a shadow, while the god who will have brought this about shall have quiet and shall rest, not for a long while indeed for a god, but for such time as would be reasonable for a man who falls asleep. Such is the mythology of the Magians.' [28]

There are number of texts by Greek and Persian writers that reflect this battle, for example in addition to those mentioned already, the Persian Pahlavi texts states in context of a heretical sect called Zurvanism, an offshoot from Zoroastrianism:

When nothing existed at all, neither heaven nor earth, the great god Zurvan (Infinite Time) alone existed, whose name means 'fate' or 'fortune'. He offered sacrifice for a thousand years that perchance he might have a son who should be called Ohrmazd (Ahura Mazda or Hormozd) and who would create heaven and earth. At the end of this period of a thousand years he began to ponder and said to himself: "What use is this sacrifice that I am offering, and will I really have a son called Ohrmazd, or am I taking all this trouble in vain?" And no sooner had this thought occurred to him then both Ohrmazd and Ahriman were conceived - Ohrmazd because of the sacrifice he had offered, and Ahriman because of his doubt. When he realized that there were two sons in the womb, he made a vow saying: "Whichever of the two shall come to me first, him will I make king." Ohrmazd was apprised of his father's thought and revealed it to Ahriman. When Ahriman heard this, he ripped the womb open, emerged, and advanced towards his father. Zurvan, seeing him, asked him: "Who art thou?" And he replied: "I am thy son, Ohrmazd." And Zurvan said: "My son is light and fragrant, but thou art dark and stinking." And he wept most bitterly.

---

[28] (Trans. J.Gwyn Griffiths, Plurarch's De Iside et Osiride, ch 46, pp193-5). As quoted by Mary Boyce textual sources for the study of Zoroastrianism. The University of Chicago press, 1990, p96-97.

And as they were talking together, Ohrmazd was born in his turn, light and fragrant; and Zurvan, seeing him, knew that it was his son Ohrmazd for whom he had offered sacrifice. Taking the barsom twigs he held in his hands with which he had been sacrificing, he gave them to Ohrmazd and said: "Up till now it is I who have offered thee sacrifice; from now on shalt thou sacrifice to me." But even as Zurvan handed the sacrificial twigs to Ohrmazd, Ahriman drew near and said to him: "Didst thou not vow that whichever of the sons should come to thee first, to him wouldst thou give the kingdom?" And Zurvan said to him: "O false and wicked one, the kingdom shall be granted thee for nine thousand years, but Ohrmazd have I made a king above thee, and after nine thousand years he will reign and will do everything according to his good pleasure." And Ohrmazd created the heavens and the earth and all things that are beautiful and good; but Ahriman created the demons and all that is evil and perverse. Ohrmazd created riches, Ahriman poverty.' [29]

The same polarity is also referred to in Zoroastrian text Yasna 30.3-4

'Truly there are two primal Spirits, twins renowned to be in conflict. In thought and word, in act they are two: the better and the bad. And those who act well have chosen rightly between these two, not so the evil doers. And when these two spirits first came together they created life and not-life, and how at the end Worst Existence shall be for the wicked, but (the House of) Best purpose for the just man.' [30]

---

[29] The Dawn and Twilight of Zoroastrianism, R.C. Zaehner, New York, (1961), 2003 edition p207-208. Also online at: http://www.farvardyn.com/zurvan2.php

[30] Mary Boyce 'Textual Sources for the Study of Zoroastrianism', The University of Chicago press, 1990, p35.

An example for the role of humanity in this battle can be seen in Yasht to Tir (Hymn to the star Sirius), here Angel star Sirius the bringer of rain battles the demon of drought. The people forget to make the appropriate libation and offerings to him, hence he loses the battle with demon of drought. Sirius then appeals to Ahura Mazda directly, who makes him the offering and gives him the strength to defeat drought:

'18. 'The next ten nights, O Spitama Zarathushtra! the bright and glorious Tishtrya mingles his shape with light, moving in the shape of a white, beautiful horse, with golden ears and a golden caparison. 'Here he calls for people to assemble, here he asks, saying:

"Who now will offer me the libations with the Homa and the holy meat? To whom shall I give wealth of horses, a troop of horses, and the purification of his own soul? Now I ought to receive sacrifice and prayer in the material world, by the law of excellent holiness." 'Then, O Spitama Zarathushtra! the bright and glorious Tishtrya goes down to the sea Vouru-Kasha in the shape of a white, beautiful horse, with golden ears and a golden caparison. 'But there rushes down to meet him the Daeva Apaosha, in the shape of a dark horse, black with black ears, black with a black back, black with a black tail, stamped with brands of terror. 'They meet together, hoof against hoof, O Spitama Zarathushtra! the bright and glorious Tishtrya and the Daeva Apaosha. They fight together, O Spitama Zarathushtra! for three days and three nights. And then the Daeva Apaosha proves stronger than the bright and glorious Tishtrya, he overcomes him. 'And Tishtrya flees from the sea Vouru-Kasha, as far as a Hathra's length. He cries out in woe and distress, the bright and glorious

Tishtrya: "Woe is me, O Ahura Mazda! I am in distress, O Waters and Plants! O Fate and thou, Law of the worshippers of Mazda! Men do not worship me with a sacrifice in which I am invoked by my own name, as they worship the other Yazatas with sacrifices in which they are invoked by their own names." If men had worshipped me with a sacrifice in which I had been invoked by my own name, as they worship the other Yazatas with sacrifices in which they are invoked by their own names, I should have taken to me the strength of ten horses, the strength of ten camels, the strength of ten bulls, the strength of ten mountains, the strength of ten rivers." 'Then I, Ahura Mazda, offer up to the bright and glorious Tishtrya a sacrifice in which he is invoked by his own name, and I bring him the strength of ten horses, the strength of ten camels, the strength of ten bulls, the strength of ten mountains, the strength of ten rivers. 'Then, O Spitama Zarathushtra! the bright and glorious Tishtrya goes down to the sea Vouru-Kasha in the shape of a white, beautiful horse, with golden ears and golden caparison.' But there rushes down to meet him the Daeva Apaosha in the shape of a dark horse, black with black ears, black with a black back, black with a black tail, stamped with brands of terror. 'They meet together, hoof against hoof, O Spitama Zarathushtra! the bright and glorious Tishtrya, and the Daeva Apaosha; they fight together, O Zarathushtra! till the time of noon. Then the bright and glorious Tishtrya proves stronger than the Daeva Apaosha, he overcomes him. 'Then he goes from the sea Vouru-Kasha as far as a Hathra's length: "Hail!" cries the bright and glorious Tishtrya."Hail unto me, O Ahura Mazda! Hail unto you, O waters and plants! Hail, O Law of the worshippers of Mazda! Hail will it be unto you, O lands! The life of the waters will flow down unrestrained to the big-seeded corn fields, to the small-seeded pasture-fields, and to the whole of the material world!'*¹²³¹*

Another figure that appears in the this cycle is figure demoness Jahi or Jeh the whore, who is the only demon that manages to wake Ahriman from his 3000 years of sleep. In the Zoroastrian text Bundahishn the story is written and she is rewarded for her success in rising Ahriman:

*'And, again, the wicked Jeh shouted thus: 'Rise up, thou father of us! for in that conflict I will shed thus much vexation on the righteous man and the laboring ox that, through my deeds, life will not be wanted, and I will destroy their living souls (nismo); I will vex the water, I will vex the plants, I will vex the fire of Ohrmazd, I will make the whole creation of Ohrmazd vexed.' And she so recounted those evil deeds a second time, that the evil spirit was delighted and started up from that confusion; and he kissed Jeh upon the head, and the pollution which they call menstruation became apparent in Jeh. He shouted to Jeh thus: 'What is thy wish? so that I may give it thee.' And Jeh shouted to the evil spirit thus: 'A man is the wish, so give it to me.' The form of the evil spirit was a log-like lizard's (vazak) body, and he appeared a young man of fifteen years to Jeh, and that brought the thoughts of Jeh to him.'*³²

The greatest demon created by Ahriman is the Azi Dahâka –the dragon, who is a three headed dragon who later in the book

---

[31] Tishtar Yasht (Hymn to the Star Sirius), AVESTA: KHORDA AVESTA (Book of Common Prayer) Translation by James Darmesteter (From Sacred Books of the East, American Edition, 1898.) http://www.sacred-texts.com/zor/sbe23/ka.htm

[32] The Bundahishn (Creation), or Knowledge from the Zand Translated by E. W. West, from Sacred Books of the East, volume 5, Oxford University Press, 1897. http://www.avesta.org/pahlavi/bund1.html#chapter3

Shahnameh (the book of kings) becomes Zahak. Zahak is a evil king with a serpent on each of his shoulders, which he has to be feed with human brains every day. In earlier Zoroastrian versions of the story (Yasht 19, 50), Atar, the lord of fire and son of Ahura Mazda attacks the dragon Azi Dahâka. He tells the dragon: *'There give it up to me thou three-mouthed Azi Dahâka. If thou seizest that Glory that cannot be forcibly seized, then I will enter thy hinder part, I will blaze up in thy jaws, so that thou mayest never more rush upon the earth made by Mazda and destroy the world of the good principle. Then Azi took back his hands, as the instinct of life prevailed, so much had Âtar affrighted him.'* [33]

The Persian dragon slayer is Thraêtaona who defeats Azi Dahâka by binding him and imprisoning him deep in a mountain top. To achieve this Thraêtaona makes many offerings to the goddess Drvâspa whose name means 'with solid horses' and is probably linked to the sea goddess Anahita as they both share similar characteristics. It is with the backing of the goddess Drvâspa that Thraêtaona wins against the dragon. In Yasht 9 we read: *"To her did Thraêtaona, the heir of the valiant Âthwya clan, offer up a sacrifice in the four-cornered Varena, with a hundred male horses, a thousand oxen, ten thousand lambs, and with an offering of libations:'Grant me this boon, O good, most beneficent Drvâspa! that I may overcome Azi Dahâka, the three-mouthed, the three-headed, the six-eyed, who has a thousand senses, that most powerful, fiendish Drug, that demon, baleful to the world, the strongest Drug that Angra Mainyu created against the material world, to destroy the world of the good*

---

[33] Yasht 19, 50. The Zend Avesta, Part II (SBE23), James Darmesteter, tr. (1882). http://www.sacred-texts.com/zor/sbe23/sbe2324.htm

principle; and that I may deliver his two wives, Savanghavâk and Erenavâk, who are the fairest of body amongst women, and the most wonderful creatures in the world. The powerful Drvâspa, made by Mazda, the holy Drvâspa, the maintainer, granted him that boon, as he was offering up libations, giving gifts, sacrificing, and entreating that she would grant him that boon.'[34] The dragon is defeated, but not slayed, he is kept captive in the Mount Davamand until the end of the world.

There are many more angels and demons in Zoroastrianism than mentioned here, there is also a class of lesser demons called the Pairakas, who are female and can take many forms, and are akin to European fairy figures.

In the Menog-i Khrad (The Spirit of Wisdom) text the angels and demons the dead person soul's meet at the Chinvat Bridge are described. The soul of a person is represented as a maiden whose appearance depends on ones deeds:

'110. Thou should not become presumptuous through life; for death comes upon thee at last, the dog and the bird lacerate the corpse, and the perishable part (sejinako) falls to the ground. During three days and nights the soul sits at the crown of the head of the body. And the fourth day, in the light of dawn with the cooperation of Sraosha the righteous, Vae the good, and Warharan the strong, the opposition of Astwihad, Vae the bad, Frazishto the demon, and Nizishto the demon, and the evil-designing action of Eshm, the evil-doer, the impetuous assailant it goes up to the awful, lofty Chinvat bridge, to which every one, righteous and wicked, is coming. And many opponents have watched there, with

---

[34] Yasht 9, 13-15. The Zend Avesta, Part II (SBE23), James Darmesteter, tr. (1882).

the desire of evil of Eshm, the impetuous assailant, and of Astwihad who devours creatures of every kind and knows no satiety, and the mediation of Sraosha (Obedience), Mithra (Covenant) and Rashnu (Justice) and the weighing of Rashnu, the just, with the balance of the spirits, which renders no favor on any side, neither for the righteous nor yet the wicked, neither for the lords nor yet the monarchs. As much as a hair's breadth it will not turn, and has no partiality; and he who is a lord and monarch it considers equally, in its decision, with him who is the least of mankind.

'And when a soul of the righteous passes upon that bridge, the width of the bridge becomes as it were a league (parasang), and the righteous soul passes over with the cooperation of Sraosha the righteous. And his own deeds of a virtuous kind come to meet him in the form of a maiden, who is handsomer and better than every maiden in the world.' [35] If the person had performed evil deeds then the reverse occurs at the Chinvat Bridge; Vizaresh, the demon, drags the person to the inevitable House of Lies (hell) and the person is greeted by a vile and hideous maiden who is the manifestation of their bad deeds.

It is easy to see why Zoroastrianism is seen as the prototype to much of Judaism, Christianity and Islam, which leads the scholar Mary Boyce to state: *'Zoroaster was thus the first to teach the doctrines of an individual judgment, Heaven and Hell, the future resurrection of the body, the general Last Judgment, and life everlasting for the reunited soul and body. These doctrines were to become familiar articles of faith to much of mankind, through*

---

[35] Menog-i Khrad (The Spirit of Wisdom) Translated by E. W. West, from Sacred Books of the East, volume 24, Oxford University Press, 1885.
http://www.avesta.org/mp/mx.html#chapter2

borrowings by Judaism, Christianity and Islam; yet it is in Zoroastrianism itself that they have their fullest logical coherence....' [36]

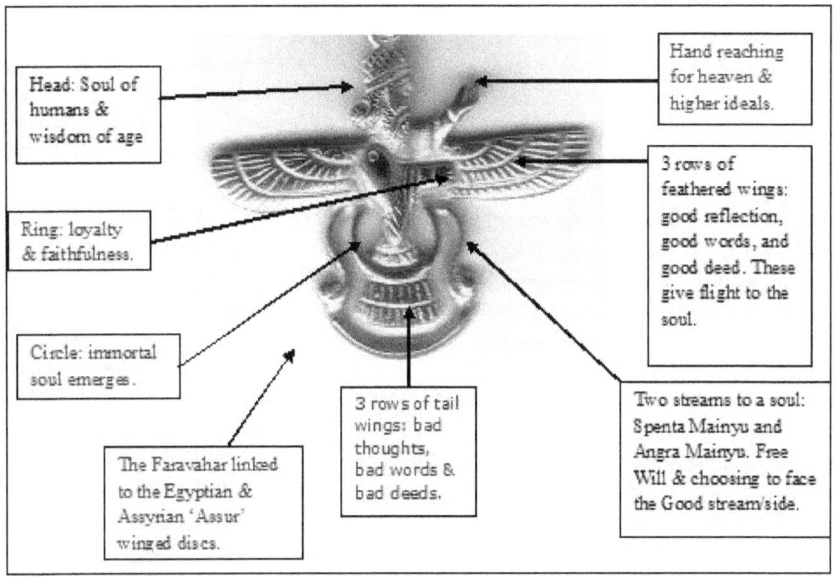

Figure 11: The meaning of the Faravahar or the Holy Guardian Angel [37]

Acknowledgements:

I would like to thank Katherine Sutherland, Parviz Varjavand, Dina G McIntyre and Zaneta Garratt for their helpful comments.

---

[36] Mary Boyce, Op. Cit. p. 29. http://www.avesta.org/avesta.html

[37] For further details see : http://www.crystalinks.com/faravahar.html & http://altreligion.about.com/od/symbols/a/faravahar.htm

Further Readings:

Traditions of the Magi: Zoroastrianism in Greek and Latin Literature (Religions in the Graeco-Roman World) by Albert F.De Jong, (Brill, 1997).

The Dawn and Twilight of Zoroastrianism, R.C. Zaehner, New York, (1961), 2003 edition.

'Textual Sources for the Study of Zoroastrianism', Mary Boyce, The University of Chicago press, 1990.

Shahnameh: The Persian Book of Kings by Abolqasem Ferdowsi, (Penguin Classics Deluxe Editions, 2007).

To be read in conjunction with *Epic and Sedition: The Case of Ferdowsi's Shahnameh* by Dick Davis (Mage Publishers, 2006).

Mithras and the right handed handshake of the Gods

This was written in 2008 and first published in Mithras Reader Vol 2, Web of Wyrd Press.

The debate about the origins of the Roman Mithras continues, and, while it is clear that the Roman Cult of Mithras was a syncretic religion using elements of Greek, Roman, and Persian cultures; it is less clear how influential different elements were in the production of the final Roman Cult. One aspect worth considering in the debate is the parallel between the act of the handshake, as seen in both the Persian Mithra and the Roman Mithras traditions. In modern times, shaking hands with the right hand is generally viewed as a sign of trust, as it shows no weapon is being held in the weapon bearing hand.

The oldest forms of handshakes were practiced by Babylonian Kings c. 1800 BCE, who had to 'take the hands of Marduk' before assuming the throne. According to Sir J. Frazer in *The Golden Bough*: 'At Babylon, within historical times, the tenure of the Kingly office was in practice lifelong, yet in theory it would seem to have been merely annual. For every year at the festival of Zagmuk the king had to renew his power by seizing the hands of the image of Marduk in his great temple of Esagil at Babylon. Even when Babylon passed under the power of Assyria, the monarchs of that country were expected to legalise their claim to the throne every year by coming to Babylon and performing the ancient ceremony at the New Year festival."[38]

Figure 12: Another example Babylonian handshake is seen in the figure of Marduk-zakir-shumi of Babylon 703 BC (right) and Shalmaneser III (left) enacting a peace pact by shaking their right hands.[39]

The earliest mention of Mithra is on a 14th century BCE clay tablet, where he is the guarantor of an agreement between the

---

[38] http://www.sacred-texts.com/pag/frazer/gb02403.htm

[39] http://prophetess.lstc.edu/~rklein/images/shalthe3.jpg reproduced here with kind permission of Prof Ralph W.Klein.

Hittites and Mitanni. Mithra is the god of contracts and agreement, his name in Avestan means Treaty or Contract.

Antiochus I of Commagene, c.69 to c.31 BCE, on the Nemrud Dagh is shown **shaking his right hand with Mithra's right hand**. Mithra has his radiant crown and his Phrygian looking cap and cloak on his shoulders. Mithra in his left hand holds the *Barsom* the sacred twigs, as he is described as doing in the Zoroastrian Avesta. This right handed hand-shake between the King and Mithra back in ca50 BCE might seem trivial at first, after all Antiochus I also shakes hands with other deities at Nemrud Dagh including Ahura Mazda as well as Mithra. However, Mithra means 'contract'; he is the god of agreements and oaths, a point also mentioned by Professor Clauss: 'Mithra was god of the oath, protector of oaths. He was god of good faith, of agreements, of loyalty. Plutarch has an anecdote of how the Great King reminded one of his servants that he had bound himself to loyalty by **shaking hands** and by swearing by Mithra: Tell me (the truth), keeping faith with the light of Mithra and the King's **right hand**' (*Vit Alex 30.8*).
[40]

---

[40] Manfred Clauss, The Roman Cult of Mithras: The God and His Mysteries (Edinburgh, Scotland: Edinburgh University Press, 2000), p4.

Figure 13: King Antiochus and Mithra. Bas-relief of the colossal temple built by Antiochus I. of Commagene, 69-31 BCE, on the Nemrud Dagh, in the Taurus Mountains. (From The Mysteries of Mithra, by Franz Cumont.)[41]

---

[41] The Mysteries of Mithra, by Franz Cumont. New York: Dover, 1956. [Originally published in 1903 by Open Court Publishing, London.] Also available online: http://www.sacred-texts.com/cla/mom/

Figure 14: King Antiochus and Ahura-Mazda. Bas-relief of the temple of Antiochus I. of Commagene, 69-34 BCE., on the Nemrud Dagh, in the Taurus Mountains. (From The Mysteries of Mithra, by Franz Cumont.) [42]

---

[42] The Mysteries of Mithra, by Franz Cumont. New York: Dover, 1956. [Originally published in 1903 by Open Court Publishing, London.]

Figure 15: Relief from Taq-e Bostan near Kermanshah, Iran. Photo by Philippe Chavin. [43]

This relief from Taq-e Bostan near Kermanshah, Iran, showing the investiture scene of Ardashir II (379–383 CE) of the Sasanian Empire. In middle the king is being given the right to rule, the divine kingship by Ahura Mazda, who hands the diadem with his right hand to the king's right hand. The two stand on a prostrate enemy. On the left is Mithra, wearing a crown of sun-rays, holding holy barsom twigs, and standing on a sacred lotus flower, he is also

---

[43] http://commons.wikimedia.org/wiki/Image:Taq-e_Bostan_-_High-relief_of_Ardeshir_II_investiture.jpg Photo by 'Philippe Chavin' reproduced here with his kind permission.

giving his blessings to his rule. One of duties of Mithra was to protect the Kingly Fortune or Divine Glory (*khvarnah* or *Farr*). The hymn to Mithra (Yasht 10) speaks of the divinity as the bestower of *khvarnah*.

The above examples show how in the ancient Middle Eastern Empires, the shaking of hands with the gods allowed the divine right of Kingship to be bestowed on the Kings by physical contact with a representation of the deity. This is a divine contract being formed when the handshake takes place, be it a peace treaty or the giving of the right to rule. The act transforms the person to stand in line with the Gods.

The divine handshake is taken from the Persian Mithra to the Roman Mithras; however, before examining this there are several other examples of right handed handshakes that need to be examined.

An example kindly provided by Dorjegiza is from the poem of Parmenides (5th century BCE), this is part of an initiate's journey from darkness to light, while in a chariot, in the company of the daughters of the Sun, he eventually reaches a temple of an unnamed goddess who enters into dialogue with him:

'(Line 20) sockets fastened with rivets and nails. Straight through them, on the broad way, did the maidens guide the horses and the car, and the goddess greeted me kindly, and took **my right hand in hers,** and spake to me these words:

Welcome, noble youth, that comest to my abode on the car

that bears thee tended by immortal charioteers!'

-English translation by John Burnet (1892)[44]

Another example kindly provided Capanellius is a portrayal of Isis receiving Io with a right handed handshake (Temple of Isis, Pompeii)[8]

'Having thus settled in Egypt, Io made a statue of Demeter, and this goddess was then called Isis. And after that, the Egyptians also gave Io the name Isis, and Io-Isis, they say, was made a Goddess by Zeus.'[45]

The handshake links the two Goddesses together, in a way a contract is formed, and they are now Io-Isis.

The paper *The Significance of the Handshake Motif in Classical Funerary Art* by Glenys Davies (American Journal of Archaeology, Vol. 89, No. 4. (Oct., 1985), pp. 627-640) provides further examples: 'The handshake appears in mythological scenes on a number of vases of the Archaic and Classical period. Many such scenes of the late archaic period involve Herakles: he is shown shaking hands with Athena on both black- and red-figure vases where the scene represents the acceptance of Herakles as an equal by the gods, and,

---

[44] English translation by John Burnet (1892) http://philoctetes.free.fr/parmenidesunicode.htm

[45] http://www.maicar.com/GML/Io.html

in particular, his comradeship with Athena. Slightly later, as one might expect, the focus switches from Herakles to Theseus. On Early Classical red-figure vases Theseus is represented linking right hands with his father, Poseidon, again presumably to indicate Theseus' exalted status......The handshake also appears in the background of two paintings of the rescue of Andromeda, between Perseus and Andromeda's father Cepheu... and ... There are also sporadic examples of the *dextrarum iunctio* used to link the deceased with his/her psychopompo as on a wall painting from Iserniag where the deceased is shown shaking hands with Mercury. The idea that the psychopompos leads the dead to a better life with the *dextrarum iunctio* is more explicitly stated in a painting in the tomb of Vibia on the Via Latinaos: there, a "good angel" leads Vibia by the right hand through an archway to the banquet of the blessed.....When used in a funerary context the handshake seems to have been associated especially with Hercules as a rescuing hero, and, to a lesser extent, with Mercury as psychopompos.'[46]

To come back to the divine handshake being taken from the Persian Mithra to the Roman Mithras, the Mithraic handshake was part of the initiatory rite, an act that connected the initiates to Mithras as well as fellow initiates.

---

[46] The Significance of the Handshake Motif in Classical Funerary Art by Glenys Davies (American Journal of Archaeology, Vol. 89, No. 4. (Oct., 1985), pp. 627-640.

Figure 16: Bas-relief fragment from Virunum in central Europe. (From The Mysteries of Mithra, by Franz Cumont.) [47]

---

[47] The Mysteries of Mithra, by Franz Cumont. New York: Dover, 1956. [Originally published in 1903 by Open Court Publishing, London.]

The Bas-relief fragment from Virunum in central Europe, shows scenes from Mithras' life, including (from bottom to top): smiting the rock from which the water flowed; holding the leg of the bull in his right hand and placing his left on Sun's head, the investiture of the Sun with his halo; Mithras and Sun **shaking right hands**; Mithras and the Sun in the chariot, showing their ascension to the sky.

Figure 17: Grand Mithraic bas-relief of Heddernheim, Germany. (From The Mysteries of Mithra, by Franz Cumont.) The investiture scene towards the top right shows Mithras and the Sun shaking right hands while sun is kneeling.

Mithra is described as the Lord of wide pastures, the lord of truth and contracts. The custom of shaking hands when greeting a friend or after a business deal perhaps originated from the religious mysteries, as a sign of not carrying a weapon, and of trust. The depiction of Mithra shaking hands (right hands) with the Syrian King Antiochus in the first century BCE, is as a sign of the transfer of divine power from God to his earthly representative and sealing the divine 'contract'. In the Roman cult of Mithras, a number of reliefs show Mithras and Sol shaking their right hands (dexiosis); and Mithraic initiates were termed *syndexioi*, 'those who have been united by a handshake' (with the Father). The handshake is also mentioned in Proficentius's poem from Rome, on the occasion of building his Mithraeum:

'This spot is blessed, holy, observant and bounteous:

Mithras marked it, and made known to

Proficentius, Father of the mysteries,

That he should build and dedicate a Cave to him;

And he has accomplished swiftly, tirelessly, this dear task

That under such protection he began, desirous

That the **Hand-shaken** might make their vows joyfully forever.

These poor lines Proficentius composed,

Most worth Father of Mithras'. [48]

The Christian writer Firmicus Maternus (fourth century CE) referred to a Roman follower of Mithras as *mysta booklopies, syndexie patros agauou* (initiate of cattle-rustling, companion by **handclasp** of an illustrious father). -Marvin Meyer, *The Ancient Mysteries: A Sourcebook of Sacred Texts* [49]

In the Mithras Liturgy we read about Mithras as having 'a bright appearance, youthful, golden-haired, with a white tunic and a golden crown and trousers, and holding **in his right hand** a golden shoulder of a young bull: this is the Bear which moves and turns heaven around, moving upward and downward in accordance with the hour.' [50]

The right hand of Mithras moves the heavens, confers 'Divine Glory' to Kings and initiates of his mysteries, and binds them in a divine contract with the gods. The Mithraic handshake was a spiritual seal of agreement and the transfer of an initiatory line. The idea is seen in the Roman cult of Mithras with the same significance and connotations as the Persian Mithra.

---

[48] Manfred Clauss, The Roman Cult of Mithras: The God and His Mysteries (Edinburgh, Scotland: Edinburgh University Press, 2000), p42.

[49] Marvin Meyer, The Ancient Mysteries: A Sourcebook of Sacred Texts (Philadelphia: University of Pennsylvania Press, 1987), p208.

[50] Marvin Meyer, The Ancient Mysteries: A Sourcebook of Sacred Texts (Philadelphia: University of Pennsylvania Press, 1987), p218.

We see this act of the divine right handed handshake down the ages, in Babylonian, Assyrian, Hittites, Mitanni, Commagene, Persian, Greek, Egyptian, and Roman religions.

It is worth noting that there are many initiatory systems still in practice today which use the right handed handshake as part of their mysteries. For example, the Freemasons and some Sufis have their own special right-handed handshake as part of their initiation and becoming part of the initiatory line. This of course is the connection with the magical 'right-hand path' (the right hand pillar on the Kabbalistic Tree of Life and the RHP in Hinduism) and its deeper meaning of having shaken the right hand of the gods and becoming connected to the gods. The act of handshaking in business meetings is perhaps the most popular sign of a Mithraic act (lord of the contract) surviving to the modern day.

Influences of Freemasonry and Sufism on Wicca and Neo-Paganism

This was written in 2010 and the Freemasonry section of the essay was submitted for Norman B. Spencer Prize collection organised by *Quatuor Coronati Lodge*.

Introduction

'Shall the folly of idiots, and the malice of the scornful, so much prevail that he who seeketh no worldly gain or glory at their hands...but only for god the treasure of heavenly wisdom and knowledge....be condemned as a companion of hellhounds, and a caller, and conjuror of wicked and damned spirits?'

- Dr. John Dee, Mathematical Praeface

Wicca and Freemasonry; on the face of it nothing can be further apart: Wicca is a Goddess/God centric neo-pagan mystery school whose Rede is 'An it harm none do what ye Will', while Freemasonry is a brotherhood and a system of morality veiled in allegory, taught in a symbolic language, whose great principles are brotherly love, relief and truth. However, as we delve deeper, the level of influence of Freemasonry on Wicca becomes apparent. This is of social and anthropological significance, as Wicca perhaps is the only religion and mystery school that was born in Britain in the 20th century, and exported to other countries; it has been growing rapidly in the wider world ever since. Wicca is one of fastest growing religions in UK and the US. In US one poll estimated the number of Wiccan and neo-pagans as 768,400. In 2001 UK national censuses there were near 80,000 pagans (Wiccan, Druid, etc...) making it seventh largest religion in UK, while the latest estimates are about five times that number (400,000). For example the summer solstice celebration at Stonehenge is attracting more and more people each year (35,000 at 2009). There are currently approximately 330,000 Freemasons in England alone which is a significant drop since its twentieth century peak in the 1950s. One Freemason writer describes this as: 'Lower membership numbers are a fact of life. Every since the 1970s and the near-total inability of the Craft to attract the "lost generation" of baby boomers (sons of our older members, fathers of our younger members), our membership curve has been heading for the basement, with little or no recovery predicted'[51]

What I propose in this essay is the perception of general decline of interest in Freemasonry should be re-examined in this light, while Freemasonry might be on a decline in the last few decades, its decedents are on an incline.

There has been a plethora of academic research into the origins of neo-paganism in last few years, and, many of the 'truths' about paganism have been shattered. The purpose of this essay is to review the published work on the history of neo-paganism and examine the evidence in the context of Freemasonry, followed by

---

[51] http://www.masonicdictionary.com/dues2.html

some thoughts on the potential effects of Sufism on Western magical orders.

The primary audience for this essay are Freemasons, who are not familiar with Wicca and the neo-pagan revival. The secondary audience are new Wiccans who may not be aware of the historical links of their chosen mystery school to Freemasonry. The essay is not aimed at Wiccan elders or experienced neo-pagans who are already aware of the links.

Hermetic Order of the Golden Dawn

What sparked the writing of this essay was my last visit to the world renowned Witchcraft Museum in Boscastle Cornwall, England. There was an object that caught my attention (Fig 18). In the Hermetic Order of the Golden Dawn section of the museum, there is an original summons (invite) to Urania Lodge no 3 of Golden Dawn. The summons is for men and women members to attend a ceremony on 21st July 1894, which is from the early days of the Golden Dawn (founded circa 1888). The venue of the meeting was the Freemasons' hall in Queen Street, London. The summons significantly also show women were performing rites in the hall as two Sorors (sisters) are named. It is an interesting piece of history as it firmly demonstrates the link between the Golden Dawn and Freemasonry; as the Golden Dawn founders were Freemasons and used to meet in the Halls. Another fascinating thing about this item was the details written about the artefact by the Witchcraft Museum

79

(Fig 19). It read something like: Wicca and Freemasonry are linked and have much in common, however due to secrecy in both systems we can't detail them.

This sparked an interest in me to find out what the links are, and indeed why the Museum, which is has been in operation for years, still thinks it has to be kept a secret.

ORDER OF THE

G. D.

IN THE OUTER.

ISIS-URANIA TEMPLE, No. 3.

V. H. Frater S'Rioghail Mo Dhream 5°=6°, Imperator.
V. H. Soror Sapientia Sapienti Dona Data 5°=6°, Præmonstrator.
V. H. Frater Levavi Oculos 5°=6°, Cancellarius.

V. H. Frater Resurgam 5°=6°, Sub-Imperator.
V. H. Soror Fortiter et Recte 5°=6°, Sub-Præmonstrator.
V. H. Frater Fide 5°=6°, Sub-Cancellarius.

You are requested to be present at
Mark Masons' Hall, Great Queen Street, W.C.

on........................the..............day of......................189......

The Temple will be opened in—

   the 0 = 0 grade at ....p.m.

   ,, 1 = 10 grade at ....p.m.

   ,, 2 = 9 grade at ....p.m.

   ,, 3 = 8 grade at ....p.m.

   ,, 4 = 7 grade at ....p.m.

The Ceremony of the Equinox..p.m.

The Temple will be closed.

L. O. Cancellarius.

    c/o P. W. BULLOCK, Esq.,
        22, Upper George Street,
            London, W.

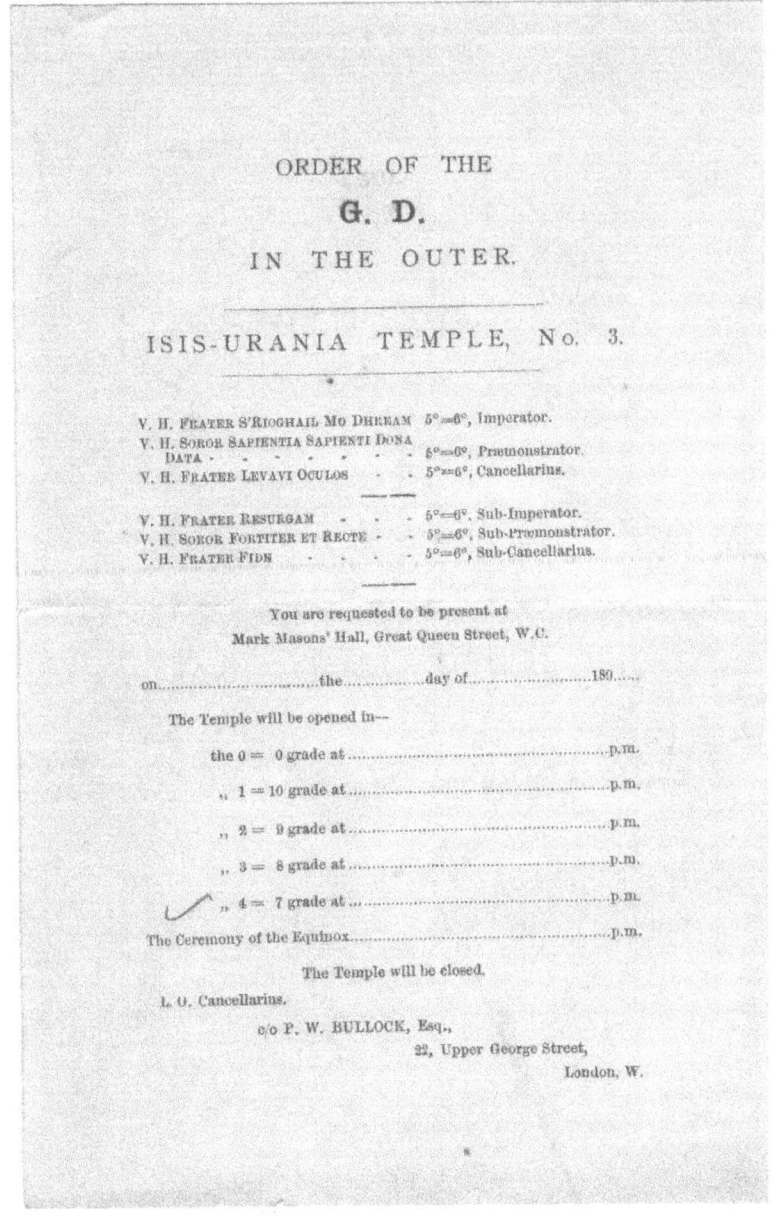

Figure 18: Golden Dawn summons to meet at the Freemason Hall, this item and below text sparked the writing of this chapter. Image kindly provided by Witchcraft Museum, Boscastle, Cornwall. For clarity image is produced twice at different settings.

Freemasonry and Witchcraft

There are many aspects of ritual and magic that link Freemasonry and witchcraft.

The three degrees of Wiccan witchcraft involve rituals that are very similar to the Masonic degrees. The use of cords and a ritual death and resurrection are particularly striking examples.

Expressions like "So mote it be" are common to both Wiccan and Masonic ritual.

We are unable to elaborate on the similarities of ritual without betraying trust. Visitors wishing to study this link will find no shortage of publications on Masonic and Wiccan ritual.

Many of the symbols used by witches are also used by Freemasons - there is a large pentagram set into the floor in the entrance to Freemasons Hall. It was the Masons that carved the Greenmen and Sheela-na-gigs in churches.

The higher degrees of Freemasonry recall many of the ancient magical mystery cults including the Rose Croix, the Knights Templar and The Royal Arch. Mysteries from the "Key of Solomon" and the Qabalah are incorporated in Wiccan Ritual, Masonic Ritual and by The Golden Dawn.

Figure 19: The text written by Witchcraft Museum, in the Golden Dawn section of the Museum. Image kindly provided by Witchcraft Museum, Boscastle, Cornwall.

The Muse of this Museum (a shrine of the Muses) inspired me to follow these bread crumbs, and led to the visiting the Muse in Freemasons Museum in London, this piece is the result of the these studies. The sources of my study are the works of Professor Ronald Hutton, Philip Hestleton, Frederic Lamond, David Rankine & Sorita D'Este, Michael Howard, and a number of other researchers in history of modern Wicca, Paganism and Freemasonry. A full list of bibliography is included at the end of this essay. In addition to these, Freemasons' Museum and library sources (located in Queen Street London) were also studied, as this is where Hermetic Order of the Golden Dawn originally met, and this venue could perhaps be seen as the birth place of many 20th century esoteric schools. It was within these hallowed halls of the Freemasons' Hall where the first rites of the Isis-Urania Lodge of the Golden Dawn were performed by its Master Mason founders. The current building is the third building on the site, built between 1927–1932; the second building was built in c.1860 and first building in 1776. Hence, the rooms where the Golden Dawn met in late 1800's no longer exist in their original form. The precursor to the Golden Dawn was Societas Rosicruciana in Anglia (SRA, the Rosicrucian Society of England) which was founded in 1865 by two Freemasons; and only Master Masons were allowed to join. The SRA was founded on the basis of manuscripts that were allegedly discovered in the vaults of the Freemasons' Hall. While there is much debate about sources of the SRA and the Golden Dawn manuscripts and texts (they were probably all written in late 1800's), one thing is clear, the Freemasons' hall in Great Queen Street, London, where the initial rituals of the Golden Dawn took place, is the physical location where the modern occult and pagan revival began; a place which perhaps should be part of the modern occultist's 'pilgrimage' tour sites!

At the street entrance of the Library and Freemason Museum at the Freemasons' hall, a large pentagram decorates the floor, a symbol significant to many mystery schools including Wicca, Druidry, the Golden Dawn and Freemasonry. The pentagram is now the official religious icon of Wicca, and in US military graveyards fallen American Wiccan soldiers have a pentagram carved on their graves, instead of a cross.

It is with the image of pentagram in mind we begin this piece and enter the mysteries.

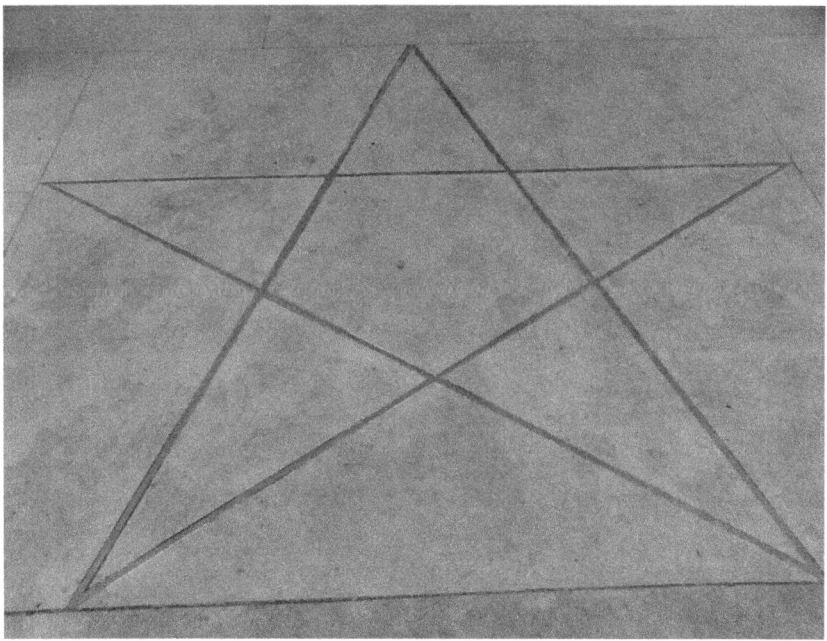

Figure 20: On the pavement outside of the 'Library and Freemasons Museum' at the Freemasons' hall, London. Photo by P. Nabarz.

A Rough Guide to Wicca's Herstory

In this essay a short summary of Wicca is presented. Turning the clock back to the late 19th early 20th centuries, when Wicca and the neo-pagan movement began, some of the texts that influenced it were taken literally. For example, the anthropologist Margaret Murray's main work the *'Witch Cult of Western Europe'*, published in 192,1 had not yet stood the test of time, while Charles G Leland's *'Aradia, Gospel of the Witches'*, translated and published in 1899, has many differences to the new 1999 version translated by Mario Pazzaglini. Furthermore, Leyland was paying his 'witch' source for more and more material, so encouraging her to come up with information. The mythology in Aradia is of course a pseudo-Christian one, where in the book, Diana and the fallen angel Lucifer, have a child together; Aradia, the first witch.

A towering figure in early 20th century occultism was Aleister Crowley (1875 –1947), whose great contribution was the philosophy of Thelema (Will), and he described himself as the 'Great Beast'! One wonders if Thelema became popular in 1960s due to its message of doing whatever you want; a misunderstanding of what its tenet of 'Do what thou Wilt' means, and then in the late 1970s and early 1980s as the all pervasive influence of counter-culture, such as Goth, Punk and Heavy Metal music which picked up on some of its central themes. Although frowned upon by many, these remain deeply imbedded in the anthems of youth culture, and reoccur in a cyclic manner, as a cultural zeitgeist. Nevertheless, Crowley was one of the most influential characters in the neo-pagan revival, the remnants of his work can be seen in almost every neo-pagan tradition. However, most people are completely unaware that some of their material in-fact comes from Crowley's writings. Crowley eventually also became the head of a quasi Masonic order called *Ordo Templi Orients* (OTO) and was initiated into a number of irregular Freemason's lodges. In one irregular lodge in Mexico, he received the 33° in Scottish Rite Freemasonry. A copy of the Charter issued by John Yarker admitting Crowley to the highest grade (33°) of the Scottish Rite of Masonry in 1910 has been published in '*The Confessions of Aleister Crowley : An Autohagiography*'[52]. He was also initiated into a lodge based in France, the Anglo Saxon Lodge 343 (today numbered 103) which was incorporated under the French Masonic constitution in Paris.[53]

With regard to Crowley's initiation in Anglo Saxon Lodge 343 according to Martin P. Starr in his paper *Aleister Crowley: freemason!* (Ars Quatuor Coronatorum,1995): 'Crowley was initiated on the 8th October 1904, presumably passed the following month, and raised on 17 December 1904; he is listed in the 'Tableau annuel' dated 31 December 1904 with the Grand Lodge number 41210, Lodge number 54'[54]. Perhaps more importantly and bringing us to the location of Freemason Hall London: 'Crowley's initiation into

---

[52] Crowley, Aleister, Symonds, John, Grant, Kenneth, The Confessions of Aleister Crowley : An Autohagiography, Arkana; New edition , 1989, p480.

[53] A Magick Life: a biography of Aleister Crowley by Martin Booth, Coronet Books, 2000, p303.

[54] Aleister Crowley: freemason! by Bro. Martin P. Starr, 1995. Ars Quatuor Coronatorum, Transactions Of The Quatuor Coronati Lodge No. 2076 London.
http://www.freemasonry.bcy.ca/aqc/crowley.html

the grade of Neophyte of the Golden Dawn took place in the (Second) Mark Mason's Hall, Great Queen Street, on 26 November 1898. In a real sense, this was Crowley's first distant brush with Freemasonry, as the Golden Dawn was created and led by an interlocking directorate of esoterically inclined freemasons, with ritual and organizational structure closely modelled on the Craft and certain Appendant Bodies. The parallels and blatant borrowings (e.g., the sceptres of the First and Third Principals in the Holy Royal Arch are used in the Golden Dawn rituals by the 'Hierophant' and 'Hegemon) which seem so obvious to a contemporary student...'[55] There are number of photos of Aleister Crowley dressed in regalia of number of irregular lodges (e.g. see http://www.freemasonry.bcy.ca/aqc/crowley.html)

Gerald Gardner (1884-1964) was the creator and founder of Wicca, and a visionary. He may have created Wicca because of his love for a certain lady [56] and naturism. However, he was a questionable character, who would deliberately play the trickster in order to popularize Wicca, which is no older than 100 years. Gerald Gardner's link with Freemasonry goes back to his early life. When Gardner was 25, he was initiated into Freemasonry in 1900s[57], Frederic Lamond states: 'Gerald had borrowed his initiation and

---

[55] Aleister Crowley: freemason! by Bro. Martin P. Starr, 1995. Ars Quatuor Coronatorum, Transactions Of The Quatuor Coronati Lodge No. 2076 London. http://www.freemasonry.bcy.ca/aqc/crowley.html

[56] The Great Wicca Hoax - Part I, Adrian Bott, White Dragon Magazine, Lughnasa 2001.

[57] Fifty Years of Wicca, Frederic Lamond, p9, p12. Green Magic, 2004.

circle opening ritual from Freemasonry and the Greater Key of Solomon to provide some atmosphere'[58]. When Gerald Gardner met Crowley, on May Day of 1947, Crowley wrote in his diary that Gardner was a Royal Arch Freemason.[59] However, Ronald Hutton in *The Triumph of the Moon* [60] seems uncertain if Gardner had reached the very high grade of Royal Arch Freemason. Crowley gave Gardner an Ordo Templi Orients (OTO) Charter for the 4th degree 1947, and later same year raised him to the 7th degree.[61] Gardener apparently also paid Crowley for subscription for the OTO Charter.[62]

The initiation of Garderner into Freemasonry according to Michael Howard in *Modern Wicca: A History From Gerald Gardner to the Present* was: 'according to the archives of the Grand Lodge at Freemasons' Hall in London, he was initiated into the first degree as an Entered Apprentice in the Sphinx Lodge in Colombo on May 23, 1910. He was then raised to the second degree on June 20, 1910, and became a Master Mason a week later on June 27. According to the lodge's records, he resigned shortly afterwards. When Gardner met Aleister Crowley in 1947, he told him that he held the high degree of Royal Arch Mason. It is possible that he was also a Co-

---

[58] Fifty Years of Wicca, Frederic Lamond, Green Magic, 2004, p41.

[59] Gerald Gardner & the Ordo Templi Orientis, by Rodney Orpheus, Pentacle magazine, Autumn 2009, p14.

[60] The Triumph of the Moon: A History of Modern Pagan Witchcraft by Ronald Hutton, Oxford University Press, 1999, p219.

[61] Gerald Gardner & the Ordo Templi Orientis, by Rodney Orpheus, Pentacle magazine, Autumn 2009, p15.

[62] Modern Wicca: A History From Gerald Gardner to the Present, Michael Howard, Llewellyn, 2010, p77.

Mason, and, the Bracelin biography says he 'had a soft spot for the Masonic Craft, and now days feels that there are close similarities in the craft of the witches; in fact he goes so far as to say that witchcraft is the original lodge'. [63] Gardner, later in life, became a member of Crotona Fellowship, which was based on Co-Masonry and was a Rosicrucian society. It was via this group that Gardner made his links with the New Forest coven, and this set him on his way on founding Wicca.

The heroine in Gardenian Wicca was Doreen Valiente (1922-1999). I had the pleasure of hearing one her last public lectures on Wicca, she re-wrote much of the Wiccan Book of Shadows, making it more accessible to a new generation. Interestingly, she had access to a set of note books which belonged to a member of Alpha-Omega lodge of the Golden Dawn, dated from 1902-1908. These notes books contained Golden Dawn initiation rituals for the different grades and teaching materials; she incorporated these into her personal Wiccan Book of Shadows.[64]

The other player in popularising Wicca was Alex Sanders, who claimed a family tradition from his grandma and was initiated in his kitchen. He went on to form another branch of Wicca (the Alexandrian Tradition). Some online resources do suggest a link

---

[63] Modern Wicca: A History From Gerald Gardner to the Present, Llewellyn, Michael Howard, 2010, pp12-13.

[64] Modern Wicca: A History From Gerald Gardner to the Present, Michael Howard, Llewellyn, 2010, p111.

between Alex Sanders and Freemasonry; however no formal reference can be located so far, hence it is assumed his link is mere speculation. Alexandrian Wicca is heavily based on Gardenian Wicca, hence Masonic influences in the material is via Gardner and Crowley. While Sanders was not a Freemason, he is said to be have been involved with a number of quasi Masonic groups, (the Knights Templars, the Order of Saint Michael, the Order of Saint George and the Ordine Della Luna)[65] meaning that the Masonic influence on Wicca was maintained up to 1970s.

Now a word on tradition; I have seen a number of times people on E-lists state that their mystery tradition goes back all the way to the Bronze age; needless to say they get a very unpleasant hammering from lots of other people on the list, and end up hanging from a metaphorical cross. The roots of modern paganism (first wave) lie in the people who made things up and said they were representing an Old religion, and, then abused that authority. The second wave of paganism came in the 60s-70s, the free love period, an age of liberation and innocence, the time of Gurus with clay feet who knew it all, and some of justifiably angry counter culture people. Traditions rely on their stated connection to the past to justify their approach, however, this is an illusion, as each rite creates something new. It is the techniques used in rites that are old

---

[65] "Alex Sanders on Adeptness and Reincarnation: An interview with Alex Sanders, 26 November 1974 by Loriel". A Voice in the Forest: Spirit Conversations with Alex Sanders by Jimahl diFiosa, Southborough, MA: Harvest Shadows Publications. http://en.wikipedia.org/wiki/Alex_Sanders_(Wiccan)

in mystery, not the school's themselves. Mystery schools in operation today be they Freemasonry or Wicca, should not need to overly justify the history and age of their schools. Certain myths and techniques they and many other groups use work, as they have since early days of Mankind.

The oldest continuous tradition and mystery schools in the UK are perhaps Freemasonry and Druidry. In case of Druidry it is no older than 250 years, while Freemasonry could be traced to the late 1500's, or, perhaps back into medieval period when there were operative masons in Europe working as Guilds. The first Freemason Grand Lodge was established in 1717 at a meeting in Goose and Gridiron pub in London, and in 1723 its regulations and book of Constitution were published. In the UK at least, every attempt for Wicca or any other mystery school to find an older lineage or a direct lineage to ancient mystery schools, or pagan ancestors has turned out to be difficult to validate.

In the case of Druidry while there is no direct lineage to ancient Druids, there are potentially several possible attempts at Druid Revivals which make for an interesting myth-history. The first recorded attempt at a Druid revival took place in Oxford. According to Dr. Michel Raoult in the book *Druid Renaissance:* 'It is said that a grove of Druids known as Cor Emrys established in the city of Oxford in 1066 CE, this name means 'City of Ambrosia' and is rich in innuendo and invokes at the same time the Pleiades constellation, the earth's magnetism, the circle of the giants of Ambrius Hill - the megalithic astronomic calendar of Stonehenge -

the traditions of Atlantis and Hyperborea, and characters such as those in the Round Table cycle of Breton novels.'[66]

No one knows how long the 1066 grove operated, but there was a second Druid Grove which was formed in 1245 in Oxford, known as the Mount Haemus Grove. Again no one knows how long this second revival lasted, but there was a third revival at some point, as there were representatives of 'an Oxford Grove' present at the well known meeting in the Apple Tree Tavern in London on 22nd September 1717, where modern Druidry was born. The Apple Tree Tavern in London was also location in 1716 and 1717 were first Freemason meetings took place. The link between Oxford and Druidry is an interesting one, as Oxford's Albion Lodge Druid group was the group into which Winston Churchill was initiated into in 1908, seven years after initiation as a Freemason in 1901 in the 'Studholme Lodge No1591' [67]. Other historical figures who appear to be interested in both Freemasonry and Druidry include William Stukeley, John Wood the Elder, Iolo Morgannwg[68] and to some extent even William Blake. The fusion of Druidry (as viewed at the time) and Freemasonry is best seen in work of John Wood the Elder in the city of Bath's Circus buildings. Its beautiful architecture is a sacred geometry which embeds dimensions of Stonehenge combined with Freemason symbolism.

---

[66] Druid Renaissance by Philip Carr-Gomm, Thorsons, 1998, p104.

[67] Winston Churchill, a Famous Man and a Freemason by W.Bro. Yasha Beresiner http://www.freemasons-freemasonry.com/beresiner7.html

[68] Masonic Papers by Dr Andrew Prescott | Iolo Morganwg and Freemasonry.

When the Ancient Order of Druid was formed it modelled itself on Freemasonry as far organisational structure was concerned. Their first group was called 'Lodge No.1 of the Ancient Order of Druids, and equivalent to Masons Grand Lodge as the executive body of the order, to which new lodges had to apply for acceptance and registration, and which would make rules for all.'[69] This is significant as links Druidry to Freemasonry nearly 100 years before the arrival of Golden Dawn.

The Sufi and Theosophical Influence

There has been a huge influx of eastern spiritual ideals into the West for a long time. The influence of traditional ideas in Hinduism, Tantra, and Buddhism, resulted in the modern theosophical movement which can be traced back to Helena Blavatsky (1831-1891) and her teachers. Its philosophy emphasizes a knowledge of divine things or knowledge derived from insight and experience as well as intellectual study, its name it's a fusion of the Greek theos (god, divinity) and Sophia (wisdom). The influence of Buddhism and Hinduism in the West all have been discussed in at great length by many writers in the past. The influence of early 20th century Eastern mystics such as G.I. Gurdjieff, is still present today. Some Pagan writers take the eastern Sufi and theosophical influence on western paganism further back to Moorish and Saracen presences in Spain. In the *Pickingill Papers* the thinking goes

---

http://www.freemasons-freemasonry.com/prescott10.html

[69] Hutton, Ronald, The Druids: A History, Hambledon Continuum, 2007, p141.

as far as suggesting the 'black man' [70] who appeared during witches initiations may have been wandering Saracens helping to build a magical group. Idris Shah also made this point in the Coalmen chapter in his book, *The Sufis*. 'El-Aswad, the Black Man, is one of the important and mysterious figures in both Northern European and Spanish -Arab accounts of witchcraft rites in many parts of Europe'[71]. This kind of influence is hard to pin down, never-the-less it should be noted that in the tales of King Arthur and his knights of the round table there are three Saracen knights, the three brothers Sir Safir, Sir Palomides, Sir Segwarides. They have seats at the round table and play their parts in the various quests, including the Grail Quest. Sir Palomides and Sir Safir are even included in the Winchester round table. The word Safir translates as Ambassador, which makes me wonder if the he was originally a Saracen ambassador.

An interesting example of contacts between England and the Islamic world is seen in the gold coin of Offa, the King of Mercia in England (757 -July 796). The coin shows 'Offa Rex' on one side and an Islamic text from the Quran on the other, the coin is similar to a Islamic Abbasid period dinar coin. Whilst how an Islamic coin came to be minted in England remains to be fully explained, there are examples of the reverse process too; early Islamic coins imitated those used in Persian Sassanian (Zoroastrian)

---

[70] Pickingill Papers the Origins of the Gardnerian Craft, W.E. Liddel and Michael Howard (Capall Bann, 1994), p. 136.

[71] The Sufis, Idries Shah (Jonathan Cape, 1971), p179.

and Byzantine (Christian), empires. For example, some still showed the Zoroastrian fire altar on one side and the head of the Sassanian king on the other, but have Arabic text from the Quran added. The old trade routes allowed the flow of goods and all type of knowledge, and, coins were the universal language spoken by all; be they Zoroastrian, Christian, Moslem or any other faith.

Figure 21: Sir Safir is seated as the 16th Knight going clockwise from King Arthur (seat 1) in the Winchester round table. King Arthur sits with a total of 24 Knights at this round table which was built c.1290.

Another stream of Sufi influence is perhaps the troubadours, whose ideals of courtly love and poetry were an echo of Sufi poetry and devotional music.

Finally, last but not least, Knight Templars and others returning from crusades brought back with them Sufi and other eastern spiritual ideas into the Western mysteries. However, what is rarely discussed are the effects and inspirations certain Sufi thoughts had at the turn of the century in the revival of Western esoteric orders.

In *Great Satan Eblis* by Dr.J.Nurbakhsh, the views of many Sufi masters on Eblis (Lucifer) as a noble figure, is beautifully discussed. The path Eblis has taken to reach Divine union with 'Allah' can be seen by orthodox Muslims as left-hand path. In Sufism, Eblis is not seen as the God's arch adversary, Eblis because of his love for God, would not prostrate before Adam. He is a jealous lover who would rather be punished by God than share him with those of clay. The cause of his fall is not seen as pride but jealousy. Such radical ideas were taken up by western occultists; in 1910 the book entitled *The scented Garden of Abdullah the Satirist of Shiraz* (Persian: Bagh-I-Muattar Haj Abdullah Shirazi) was published. The author behind this was Aleister Crowley, who was fascinated by the Persian language and revelled in the ideas of Sufis travelled widely in Middle East as well as India. Haj-Abdullah Shirazi is a character created by Crowley, after his learning of the modern Persian language to convey his ideas based on Sufi symbols. One modern Sufi in a discussion forum described his book 'someone splattering his ego in the garden, simply pornography, which lacked anything of any depth'. I guess being able to annoy local mystics wherever he went and playing the devil's advocate, is perhaps one of the main consistencies in Crowley's life. The scented garden of Abdullah consists of 42 Ghazzals (Persian poetic verses) and short stories, some of which refer to his male lover back in Cambridge. Even a century after their first publication, due to their highly erotic nature, orthodox Muslims can see them as obscene and blasphemous. However, Crowley was not the first westerner who invented his own Sufi poet. Sir Francis Burton published in 1880 Sufi couplets of Haji Abdu El-Yezdi: *The Kasidah of Haji Abdu El-Yezdi: 'A lay of higher order'*.

There are other Sufi influences in Crowley's work too, for example his ARARITA formula (Liber DCCCXIII vel ARARITA) begins with verses (Surah 112) from the Koran:

'Qul huwallaahu ahad

Allahus samad

Lam yalid wa lam yuulad

Wa lamyakun lahuuu kufuwan ahad'

Which Crowley describes as: 'O my God! One is Thy Beginning! One is Thy Spirit, and Thy Permutation One'.

Crowley is best known for his books on Magick and his involvement in the breakage of the Hermetic Order of Golden Dawn, and his subsequent publication of their texts which led to an explosion of interest in mysticism. Members of the Hermetic order of Golden Dawn, which was founded in 1888, were already familiar with much of Eastern philosophy. The breakage of this order occurred in 1903, and its members divided into those who wanted, for a better word a left-hand path approach, and those believed in a more puritan (right hand path) approach. The puritan societies and ideas that resulted from the breakage of Hermetic order of Golden Dawn have become to be known as the Western Mysteries. These groups subscribe to the mystery traditions of Egypt and Eleusis as well as those of involving Druid and sometimes Kabalistic thinking. These groups paved the way for the sudden rise of interest in mysticism in the Hippy era.

In Germany in 1902 the Ordo Templi Orients (Order of the Oriental Templars) was founded by Karl Kellener (1851- 1905) who, during his extensive travels in the East, was initiated by the Arab Fakir Soliman Ben Aifha, and the Indian Yogis Bhima Sen Pratap and Sri Mahatma Agamya Guru Paramahamsa. The fusion of Sufism and Tantra within the OTO kept on developing. Soon, after the publication of *'Scented Garden of Abdulah'*, Aleister Crowley was contacted by the OTO and travelled to Germany and meet Theodor Reuss (1855-1923). Crowley was initiated into the OTO in 1910, after which he profoundly influenced the development of rites of the OTO.

The OTO is also an offspring of Freemasonry as all the founders were Freemasons, and, in its early days, being a Freemason was a prerequisite for entrance into its higher degrees; hence a great deal of Freemason's symbology and techniques etc are found in the rites of OTO. The OTO being a quasi Masonic organisation, meant that in its early days, Freemasons and Co-Masons could join the OTO at the same degrees they held in Freemasonry. [72]

The Sufi connection is best seen in the third degree of the OTO where instead of commemorating the murder of Hiram Abiff as Freemasonry does, in OTO the murder of Sufi master and martyr, Mansur Al Hallaj is marked. The OTO, enacts the mystery around the death of Hallaj in the same way Freemasons mark the mystery of Hiram Abiff, the Master Builder.

Hallaj was martyred on March 26, 922AD, for heresy for making statements like *Anā l-Haqq* 'I am The Truth', and 'There is nothing wrapped in my turban but God' and 'There is nothing in my cloak but God' when he was in mystical trance. These teachings of Hallaj are present in the third degree of OTO.

The development of rites by Crowley, within the OTO would be a major influence on the rites of Wicca. In the Gnostic Mass in which the space is arranged similarly to a Freemason's Lodge, a Mass takes place, which is one of the sources of the Wiccan Great Rite. This will be covered in detail later in this essay.

The left hand path (LHP) philosophy within the OTO kept on growing, and, found an even wider audience when Gerald Gardner the British founder of Wicca was initiated into the 9th grade of OTO. Gardner himself had travelled greatly in the East

---

[72] Gerald Gardner & the Ordo Templi Orientis, by Rodney Orpheus, Pentacle magazine, Autumn 2009, p.15.

and he was according to *'Witches-an encyclopaedia of paganism and magic'* by Michael Jordan was a Sufi initiate[73]. However, his being a Sufi initiate is not mentioned in Gardner biography. Gardner was also a friend of Idris Shah, the most prominent Sufi writer in the West. Idris Shah wrote Gardner's biography *'Witch'* under the alias Jack Bracelin, who was another mutual friend. It could be suggested that Shah didn't use his own name as he probably didn't want to be associated publicly with Wicca, while Jack Bracelin was already doing a great deal to catch the eye of the media. Shah's Octagon Press published Gardner's biography in 1960. Idris Shah's proposal in his classic book *'Sufis'* (1964) of the influence of Sufism on medieval Witch cults in Europe via Spain, was probably inspired by his workings with Gardner. Shah has proposed a number of potential Sufi influences on magical lore in the medieval period, to name a few: Moorish dance (or Morris dance, which is disputed), witch's athame (blood letter), Rosicrucian ideology, the Knight Templars and Baphomet.

It is fascinating that several of the central figures in the revival of neo-paganism were linked Sufism as well as Freemasonry. The influence of Sufism on paganism has still continued and can be seen in the works of Andrew Chumbly and his branch of 'Sabbatical Witchcraft'. Chumbly's book *'Qutub'* was published in 1995, and consists of 73 short gazzals. *Qutub* is Sufi word for the magical Pole, or point of spiritual orientation; and the book contains many poems

---

[73] 'Witches-an encyclopaedia of paganism and magic' by Michael Jordan Kyle Cathie Ltd, 1996, p87.

and calligraphy based on Sufism. This Sufi current in Western Magic is still being manifested, and, most recently can seen in the publication of the 'Rumi Tarot' in 2009 by Nigel Jackson in which he combines his beautiful artwork with Rumi's Sufi poetry.

A final note; when dealing with the history of esoteric material proceed with caution, there are people who really think the *Necronomicon* is an ancient text, written by Arab mage, Abdual Alhazred! This is a modern work, and like many other approaches, as mentioned before, attempts to give itself an ancient history. A question to ask for any tradition, does it work for you? Rather than how old it is. The proof is in the pudding.

To bring the topic back from Sufism to Freemasonry and fully square the circle, it is worth noting the that East-West spiritual influences are bidirectional. For example, when Freemasonry was introduced from the West to the Arab world and the Middle East in the 19th century, it was seen as a Sufi order. For example in Turkey the word rite in 'Ancient and Accepted Scottish Rite was replaced with the word *Tariqa* (Sufi path). This means it was seen as Ancient and Accepted Scottish Sufi Path.[74] The way some Sufis recognised Freemasonry as another Sufi order in the 19th century points to a number of factors: the similarity of Muslim Guilds to the original operative Stone Masons Guilds, the universality of ritual techniques

---

[74] Gnostic/Sufi Symbols and Ideas In Turkish & Persian Freemasonry and in Masonic-Inspired Organisations, by Professor Thierry Zarcone, the Canterbury papers vol5, Knowledge of the heart: Gnostic Movements and Secret Traditions, Lewis Masonic, 2006, p118.

mystery schools use, and, Chivalry orders. Professor Thierry Zarcone's work *Gnostic/Sufi Symbols and Ideas In Turkish & Persian Freemasonry and in Masonic-Inspired Organisations* is key reading in understanding this link.

Traditional Witchcraft and Wicca

Another twist in the story comes from the potential influence of Traditional Witchcraft and Hereditary practices on Wicca, for example, the role of the Essex Cunning Man George Pickingill (1816-1909). In the book *'Pickingill Papers the Origins of the Gardnerian Craft'*, by W.E. Liddel and Michael Howard (Capall Bann, 1994) a number of interesting points are made:

1. 'A small coterie of Master Masons established a lengthy and productive relationship with Pickingill from 1850's onwards. These Freemasons entertained 'Rosicrucian' fantasies and sought personal verification that Masonic Crafters and Rosicrucian Crafters were siblings of the Old religion. Old George awed these Masonic 'Rosicrucians' with demonstrations of his mastery over elements. He was also able to fascinate them by expounding 'the inner secrets' of Masonry. None of these learned Masons could comprehend how this non-Mason had penetrated their Craft mysteries. It was reluctantly conceded that the witch cult may have possessed some secret arcane

knowledge. Occult minded Freemasons were to question Old George very thoroughly over a period of many years.'[75]

2. 'It is no exaggeration to claim that Pickingill machinations materially influenced the founding of SRA 'Societas Rosicruciana in Anglia' (in 1865) and the GD 'Golden Dawn' (in 1888). Two Master Masons who were to become members of SRA had been accepted by Old George as his pupils. I allude to Hargrave Jennings and W.J. Hughan. Both men believed that the Masonic Craft could learn much of value from the witch cult. Pickingill freely exchanged ideas and Craft rituals with these two eminent pupils.'[76]

3. 'SRA was founded in 1865 by Robert Wentworth Little and he allegedly founded the Society on the basis of ancient manuscript he found in Freemason Hall. These rituals allegedly bore a resemblance to those 18th century German Rosicrucian group called the Fratres of the Golden & Rosy Cross. Membership of SRA was restricted to Master Masons…The belief that Freemasonry and Rosicrucianism had originated in the pagan religions and classical mysteries was widespread in the 19th century. C.W. Leadbeater (1847-1934), a high ranking Freemason, Co-Mason and Theosophist, for instance claimed that Masonic rites and symbols can be traced back to the

---

[75] *Pickingill Papers the Origins of the Gardnerian Craft*, W.E. Liddel and Michael Howard (Capall Bann, 1994), p37.

[76] *Pickingill Papers the Origins of the Gardnerian Craft*, W.E. Liddel and Michael Howard, p39.

mystery cults of Egypt, Crete, Greece and Rome. (Leadbeater 1926).' [77]

The system and Craft that Old George practised was said to be a combination of 'Danish paganism, Arabic mysticism, Christian heresy, and French witchcraft'.[78]

In addition to Old George, there might be other influences from Traditional Witchcraft on Wicca via other cunning men. For example, a parallel exists in the form of Mason's Word and Horseman's Word. Of course there are other threads which make up Wicca, the free festival movement, the hippy era, the Green movement, environmentalism, feminism, left wing politics, folk lore studies, archaeology, anthropology, etc... If we take the actual time lines over generations into account, one could even say that Wicca is mother of modern paganism, the Golden Dawn its grandmother, and Freemasonry its great grandmother. These threads are the central threads that helped to create modern paganism, one of fastest growing religions in UK and the US.

However, traditional witchcraft is not the subject of study here, just add a view; I did once attend a talk by Paddy Slade (who claims to be a hereditary witch). What I interpreted from her talk was that traditional and folk magic were essentially the magic you practice to help you survive where you live. In her case, it was a

---

[77] *Pickingill Papers the Origins of the Gardnerian Craft*, W.E. Liddel and Michael Howard, p41.

[78] Howard, Michael, Modern Wicca: A History From Gerald Gardner to the Present, Llewellyn, 2010, p.51.

family type cottage near a woodland etc... and she learned how to be in tune with that.

This is what I call 'survival magic' or aka instinct, and everyone does it to lesser or greater level. There are no written sources, or pantheons, or formal teaching structures or groups. You learn it from where you live and the people around you. You learn diffcrent things to become in tune with surroundings; it is different if you live by the sea, inland, in cities, in villages, or in forest etc... Survival magic is knowing your landscape so you can survive and folklore is part of it.

One should be clear about the question of lineages, if the question is, were there magical practitioners going back to 100s of years? Then yes people have always been aware of following their instinct, e.g. lay your hand for healing, rub it better, herbal healing, calling an object by someone's name and harming it as in sympathetic magic etc… If the question is, are there organised religious paganism or mystery schools and practices going back 100s of years? Then there is no evidence before 1700s. Modern paganism came out of Gardeners Wicca from 1950's, the biggest in influence on Wicca probably was the Golden Dawn (around 1888 onward) and the biggest influence on Golden Dawn was Freemasonry.

Modern paganism in structure, pantheon, formal teaching, grades etc. has a lot in common with the Golden Dawn and Freemasonry. The Golden Dawn and Freemasonry are the biggest thread; there are of course other threads in fabric of modern paganism, but they are probably less of historical influence.

Freemasonry in Wicca

The influence of Freemasonry on Wicca is twofold, first there are the direct influences, which are examined is in this essay, second are the indirect influences which are discussed in the next part of the essay. The direct influences below are actual words, steps, and ritual structures. The mental craft seen in Freemasonry applies most to Gardnerian Wicca then other neo-pagan branches. In Wicca the Charges are memorised and many ritual material are recited word perfect from memory, this feature of Wicca is also probably inherited from Freemason and is also in line with some classical pagan schools. Other branches of neo-paganism tend to read from printed scripts, or use word craft that is to create poetry, invocations and other material especially for each occasion on the spot during the rites.

The difference between mental craft and word craft as spiritual techniques is interesting. Celtic Bards and Druids, Indian Brahmin priests, Persian Zoroastrian priests and many other mystery schools required their initiates to become adept in mental craft as well as word craft and the holy texts had to be fully memorised as part of the training. These were oral traditions which used mental craft to convey the teachings. These we can see today in Freemasonry and Gardnerian Wicca.

The Craft

The Freemasonry and Wicca both are also known as 'the Craft'. The name of a 'thing' defines it; it is a basic part of the human language to name things that are linked with a similar name.

The Working Tools

In Freemasonry the term "Working Tools" is used, these for the first degree are the 24 inch rule, the common lump-hammer, and the stone cutters blade (chisel)[79]. Wicca also uses the term "Working Tools", these are usually Athame, Cup, platter (with Pentacle drawn on it), the Book, and Candle. Other items such as Wand, Bell and Incense are sometimes included.

In Freemasonry, the initiate is presented with the working tools[80], in Wicca in a similar point in the rite as part of the first degree initiation the working tools are presented and explained to the initiate: 'Now I Present to thee the Working Tools...'[81]. While the tools are different, the opening wording and timing are identical.

The Charge

There are a number of powerful and moving catechisms and teaching statements in Freemasonry that are delivered at different stages of initiation, Freemasonry refers to these statements as 'Charges'. These Charges are tools of conveying complex myths and

---

[79] Turning the Hiram Key: Making Darkness Visible by Robert Lomas, Lewis Masonic, 2007, p71.
[80] Turning the Hiram Key: Making Darkness Visible by Robert Lomas, 2007, p70.
[81] The Gardnerian Book of Shadows, by Gerald Gardner, at sacred-texts.com

stories. The oldest of these Charges is the Regius Poem or the Halliwell Manuscript, circa 1390.

In Wicca there is also a 'Charge', the 'Charge of the Goddess' which is used with a similar intent to convey a deep message, it is to be read while the initiate stands, properly prepared before the Circle. While Freemasons square the circle, Wiccan meet in a circle.

Perhaps the real spirit of Wicca is not in detail of its history but best captured in the concluding lines of Charge of the Goddess.

'The Charge: Lift Up the Veil (1949)

Magus: "Listen to the words of the Great mother, who of old was also called among men Artemis, Astarte, Dione, Melusine, Aphrodite, Cerridwen, Diana, Arianrhod, Bride, and by many other names."

High Priestess: "At mine Altars the youth of Lacedaemon in Sparta made due sacrifice. Whenever ye have need of anything, once in the month, and better it be when the moon is full, ye shall assemble in some secret place and adore the spirit of Me who am Queen of all Witcheries and magics. There ye shall assemble, ye who are fain to learn all sorcery, yet have not won its deepest secrets. To these will I teach things that are yet unknown. And ye shall be free from slavery, and as a sign that ye be really free, ye shall be naked in your rites, both men and women, and ye shall dance, sing, feast, make music, and love, all in my praise. There is a Secret Door that I have made to establish the way to taste even on earth the elixir of immortality. Say, 'Let ecstasy be mine, and joy on earth even to me, To Me,' For I am a gracious Goddess. I give unimaginable joys on earth, certainty, not faith, while in life! And upon death, peace unutterable, rest, and ecstasy, nor do I demand aught in sacrifice."

Magus: "Hear ye the words of the Star Goddess."

High Priestess: "I love you: I yearn for you: pale or purple, veiled or voluptuous. I who am all pleasure, and purple and drunkenness of the innermost senses, desire you. Put on the wings, arouse the coiled splendor within you. Come unto me, for I am the flame that burns in the heart of every man, and the core of every Star. Let it be your inmost divine self who art lost in the constant rapture of infinite joy. Let the rituals be rightly performed with joy and beauty. Remember that all acts of love and pleasure are my rituals. So let there be beauty and strength, leaping laughter, force and fire by within you. And if thou sayest, 'I have journeyed unto thee, and it availed me not,' rather shalt thou say, 'I called upon thee, and I waited patiently, and Lo, thou wast with me from the beginning,' for they that ever desired me shall ever attain me, even to the end of all desire.

This much of the rites must ever be performed to prepare for any initiation, whether of one degree or of all three.' [82]

The five points of Fellowship

In Freemasonry, the body of Master Hiram in the third degree is lifted using the posture called the Five Points of Companionship[83]

---

[82] The Gardnerian Book of Shadows, by Gerald Gardner, at sacred-texts.com

and in the third degree initiation, Freemason initiates state: 'I will defend the Five Points of Fellowship, in enactment as well as concept...'[84]

This is echoed in the Wiccan third degree with a variation: 'Make open the path of intelligence between us. For these truly are the five points of fellowship (the point-up triangle above the pentacle, the symbol for the third degree), feet to feet, knee to knee, groin to groin, breast to breast, arms around back, lips to lips, by the Great and Holy Names....'[85] In Wicca there is also a fivefold salute or fivefold kiss, which is based on this same schema:

> 'Blessed be thy feet, that have brought thee in these ways;
>
> Blessed be thy knees, that shall kneel at the sacred altar;
>
> Blessed be thy womb, without which we would not be;
>
> Blessed be thy breasts, formed in beauty and in strength;
>
> Blessed be thy lips, that shall speak the sacred names.'[86]

This is one of the reasons the pentagram is a significant symbol to both Wicca and Freemasonry as it relates to five points of fellowship, but also the four elements (earth, air, fire, water) in balance under Spirit the fifth element or the upper point of the pentagram.

---

[83] Turning the Hiram Key: Making Darkness Visible by Robert Lomas, 2007, p177.
[84] Turning the Hiram Key: Making Darkness Visible by Robert Lomas, 2007, p143.
[85] The Gardnerian Book of Shadows, by Gerald Gardner, at sacred-texts.com
[86] The Gardnerian Book of Shadows, by Gerald Gardner, at sacred-texts.com

The Apprentice Freemason wears the his white leather apron with the flap pointed upward as to 'displays all five points of the apron',[87] when the a Freemason reaches the third degree he learns more about the meaning of the pentagram: 'The four points of the crossed bones meeting in the skull at the centre symbolise the Five Points of Fellowship which bring us to the centre. Yet this solemn symbol of morality contains within it five points of hope, when illuminated by the light of the bright Morning Star rising in the east.'[88]

So Mote it Be

After recitation of Prayers and Charges in Lodges, all endorse this by saying 'so mote it be'[89]. In Wiccan groups also after prayers, invocation and charges the initiates say 'so mote it be'. This not simple case of saying 'Amen', but an specific act which is rooted in Freemasonry. It is from Freemasonry, that Wicca has inherited 'so mote it be'. Ronald Hutton placed the use of this phrase as a standard cry of endorsement for the late medieval Charge the Regius Poem.[90]

Merry Meet, Merry Part, Merry Meet Again

One of the most popular Wiccan phrases, is 'Merry Meet, Merry Part, Merry Meet Again' which is said at the end of rites, this too

---

[87] Turning the Hiram Key: Making Darkness Visible by Robert Lomas, 2007, p78.
[88] Turning the Hiram Key: Making Darkness Visible by Robert Lomas, 2007, p171.
[89] Turning the Hiram Key: Making Darkness Visible by Robert Lomas, , 2007, p47.
[90] The Triumph of the Moon: A History of Modern Pagan Witchcraft by Ronald Hutton, Oxford University Press, 1999, page 55.

has its origins in Freemasonry, in *'Wicca Magical Beginnings'* we read: 'Recording the witch trials in his book *Saducismus Triumphatus* (1681), Joseph Glanvill recorded the 1664 confession of the witch Elizabeth Styles, who said when they parted from their meetings the witches said "A boy! Merry Meet, Merry part" which may be the origin of the Merry meet, Merry Part, Merry Meet Again at the end of ceremonies. However, the words spoken at the end of the old second degree Masonic initiation could also be the root of this phrase, being "Happy have me meet, happy have we been, happy may we part, and happy meet again" '.[91]

This suggests that Gardner picked the 'merry meet' phrase from either the New Forest coven, which may had links to an older coven; or, he picked it up from his Freemason days. Freemasons in turn had picked it up from a common source that fed both the 1664 coven and freemasonry, the common source perhaps being that it was simply a popular phrase in that historical period.

The Challenge
In Freemasonry, during the first degree initiation (Entered Apprentice) a dagger is placed to the chest of the initiate as he enters the lodge. Lomas describes this as: '…dagger was presented to your naked breast, to symbolise that, had you recklessly sought to force yourself forward, you would have been the agent of your own

---

[91] Rankine, David; D'Este, Sorita, Wicca Magical Beginnings, Avalonia, 2008, p107.

demise by implement; not so, however, the Brother who held it....'[92]

In Wicca in a similar manner the initiator 'Places the point of the sword to the Postulant's breast, he says, O thou who standeth on the threshold between the pleasant world of men and the domains of the Dread Lords of the Outer Spaces, hast thou the courage to make the Assay? For I tell thee verily, it were better to rush on my weapon and perish miserably than to make the attempt with fear in thy heart.'[93]

Interestingly, a much older example of placing a sword on the chest of the initiates can been in the Mysteries of Mithras. This is shown in the trials of initiations as depicted on the walls Capua Vetere Mithraeum, Second centaury AD.

Properly Prepared

The term 'properly prepared' is use both in Freemasonry and Wicca, though there are some differences between the states of preparedness.

In Freemasonry the initiate can be seen[94] as blindfolded, a cable tow round his neck, fully clothed but a breast and knee are

---

[92] Turning the Hiram Key: Making Darkness Visible by Robert Lomas, 2007, p62.

[93] The Gardnerian Book of Shadows, by Gerald Gardner, at sacred-texts.com

[94] Lomas, Robert, The Secret Science of Masonic Initiation, Lewis Masonic, 2008. See cover for image of an initiate's dress.

exposed[95] and he has to 'travel before them to demonstrate due cause that he is properly prepared to become a Mason'.[96]

In Wicca initiates are 'Properly Prepared (1953) as: Naked, but sandals (not shoes) may be worn. For initiation, tie hands behind back, pull up to small of back, and tie ends in front of throat, leaving a cable-tow to lead by, hanging down in front. (Arms thus form a triangle at back.) When initiate is kneeling at altar, the cable-tow is tied to a ring in the altar. A short cord is tied like a garter round the initiate's left leg above the knee, with ends tucked in. Another is tied round right ankle and ends tucked in so as to be out of the way while moving about. These cords are used to tie feet together while initiate is kneeling at the altar and must be long enough to do this firmly, the knees must also be firmly tied, this must be carefully done. If the aspirant complains of pain, the bonds must be loosened slightly; always remember the object is to retard the blood flow enough to induce a trance state. This involves slight discomfort, but great discomfort prevents the trance state; so it is best to spend some little time loosening and tightening the bonds until they are just right. The aspirant alone can tell you when this is so. This, of course, does not apply to the initiation, as then no trance is desired; but for the purpose of ritual it is good that the

---

[95] Turning the Hiram Key: Making Darkness Visible by Robert Lomas, , 2007, p43.

[96] Turning the Hiram Key: Making Darkness Visible by Robert Lomas, Lewis Masonic, 2007, p47.

initiates be bound firmly enough to feel they are absolutely helpless but without discomfort.'[97]

Circumambulation

It is also worth noting that both in Freemasonry[98] and Wicca[99] the first degree initiate stands in North East during the first part of the ceremony. It is this level of detail that really highlights the influence of Freemasonry on Wicca. The north east corner is the place of sun rise at the summer solstice.

The initiate then moves to four cardinal points or the stations of the sun, in Wicca the initiate is led around the circle and proclaimed at four quarters (N, S, E, and W). In Freemasonry before the first degree initiate makes his journey, he is told:' The Brethren stationed at the various points of the compass will take note that Mr ... is about to travel before them to demonstrate due cause that he is properly prepared to become a Mason'.[100] This is repeated again: 'travelled round and round the lodge room, moving from the sunrise of the Master's chair to the meridian of the Junior Warden, to the sunset of the Senior Warden before returning via the darkness of the northern horizon.'[101]

---

[97] The Gardnerian Book of Shadows, by Gerald Gardner, at sacred-texts.com

[98] Turning the Hiram Key: Making Darkness Visible, by Robert Lomas, Lewis Masonic, 2007, p43.

[99] The Witches Way, Janet and Stewart Farrar, Hale, 1984, p16.

[100] Turning the Hiram Key: Making Darkness Visible by Robert Lomas, 2007, p47.

[101] Turning the Hiram Key: Making Darkness Visible by Robert Lomas, 2007, p66.

In Wicca the Initiator leads the initiate to the cardinal points in turn and says: Take heed, O Lords of the Watchtowers of the East, (then South, West, North) that (initiates name), is properly prepared, will be made a Priestess and a Witch. [102]

Cowan

In both Freemasonry and Wicca there are vows of secrecy and penalties associated with breaking of the vows. The non-initiates are called cowans in Freemasonry and Wicca, and secrets are protected from cowans. Similar concept is also present in other systems, for example non-initiates are called Pashu in Tantra, or in the fictional story of Harry Potter the term Muggles is used!

The Apprentice Freemason is told during his initiation about the role of the external guard of the lodge: 'he stands outside the Lodge, holding a drawn sword, to protect the Brethren from the incursions of cowans and other eavesdroppers while making sure that candidates are well prepared to become brothers among us.' [103]

The use of the term cowan in Freemasonry is very appropriate and makes senses as it refers to a dry stone-waller. According to The Oxford International Dictionary of the English Language: 'Cowan - 1598 1. Sc. One who does the work of a mason, but has not been apprenticed to the trade. 2. Hence, one uninitiated in the secrets of Freemasonry 1707. 3. slang. A sneak, eavesdropper.' And according to The Oxford English Dictionary, one who builds dry stone walls

---

[102] The Gardnerian Book of Shadows, by Gerald Gardner, at sacred-texts.com
[103] Turning the Hiram Key: Making Darkness Visible by Robert Lomas, 2007, p82.

(i.e., without mortar); a dry-stone-diker; applied derogatorily to one who does the work of a mason, but who has not been regularly apprenticed or bred to the trade.'[104]

The use of the word cowan in Wicca is a borrowing from Freemasonry which makes little contextual sense in Wicca; it is a copying of the term without appreciating its historical meaning. However, it further demonstrates the level of influence Freemasonry had on Wicca.

The Three Degrees

The Wiccan text used here is from the 1949 Wiccan Gardnerian version; this version was compiled by Aidan A. Kelly.[105] I have made a comparison to the rite of Craft Freemasonry as described in *Turning the Hiram Key: Making the Darkness Visible* by Robert Lomas (Lewis Masonic, 2007 edition). The underlined Wiccan texts below show the overlaps between Freemasonary rites as described in Lomas' book, and Wiccan rites in the Gardnerian Book of Shadows. My choice of using Lomas' text is three fold: it is an interesting book on the initiatory journey, it is a modern publication which takes into account modern development, and it is a book that appears to be approved by Freemason lodges as it is being sold at Freemason Hall Museum shop.

---

[104] http://www.masonicworld.com/EDUCATION/files/dec04/cowan.htm
[105] The Gardnerian Book of Shadows, by Gerald Gardner, at sacred-texts.com

In addition to direct influences there are also conceptual similarities between Freemasonry and Wicca. For example, coming to terms with death. In Wicca this is done in the second degree with the descent into the underworld. The myth of Persephone and Hades or Inanna journey's in the underworld is acted out, hence, in Wicca the initiate experiences a ritual death. In Freemasonry, in the third degree the initiate too goes through a ritual death, though it is focused on murder of Hiram Abiff, the ritual death is also common among many other mystery schools; however we are not covering these conceptual similarities in this essay but direct influences of Freemasonry on Wicca. The conceptual similarities that exist among mystery schools are techniques that have worked for 1000's of years and are not limited to any one religion, philosophy, or mystery school.

Initiation: First Degree

The first degree symbol in Wicca is the triangle, the second an inverted pentagram, the third upward pentagram with a triangle floating above it.

In Freemasonry the first degree wears his apron, with pointed flap set upward to show all five points of the apron too.[106]

The following is the text of the Wiccan first degree:

---

[106] Turning the Hiram Key: Making Darkness Visible, by Robert Lomas, Lewis Masonic, 2007, p78.

'Magus leaves circle by the doorway, goes to Postulant, and says, "Since there is no other brother here, <u>I must be thy sponsor</u>, as well as priest. I am about to give you a warning. If you are still of the same mind, answer it with these words: 'Perfect Love and Perfect Trust.'" <u>Placing the point of the sword to the Postulant's breast</u>, he says, "O thou who standeth on the threshold between the pleasant world of men and the domains of the Dread Lords of the Outer Spaces, hast thou the courage to make the Assay? For I tell thee verily, it were better to rush on my weapon and perish miserably than to make the attempt with fear in thy heart." Postulant: "I have <u>two Passwords</u>: Perfect Love and Perfect Trust." Magus drops the sword point, saying, "All who approach with perfect love and perfect trust are doubly welcome." Going around behind her, he blindfolds her, then putting his left arm around her waist and his right arm around her neck, he pulls her head back, says, "I give you the 3rd password, a Kiss to pass through this dread Door," and pushes her forward with his body, through the doorway and into the circle. Once inside, he releases her saying, "This is the way all are first brought into the circle." Magus closes the doorway by drawing the point of the sword across it three times, joining all three circles, saying, "Agla, Azoth, Adonai," then drawing three pentacles to seal it. Magus guides Postulant to south of altar, and whispers, "Now there is the Ordeal." Taking a short piece of cord from the altar, he ties it around her right ankle, saying, "Feet neither bound nor free." Taking a longer cord, he ties her hands together behind her back, then pulls them up, so that the arms form a triangle, and <u>ties the cord around her neck, leaving the end dangling</u>

down in front as a Cable Tow. With the Cable Tow in his left hand and the sword in his right hand, the Magus leads her sunwise around the circle to the east, where he salutes with the sword and proclaims, "Take heed, O Lords of the Watchtowers of the East, (name), properly prepared, will be made a Priestess and a Witch." Magus leads her similarly to the south, west, and north, making the proclamation at each quarter. Next, clasping Postulant around the waist with his left arm, and holding the sword erect in his right hand, he makes her circumambulate three times around the circle with a half-running, half-dancing step. He halts her at the south of the altar, and strikes eleven knells on the bell. He then kneels at her feet, saying, "In other religions the postulant kneels, as the Priests claim supreme power, but in the Art Magical, we are taught to be humble, so we kneel to welcome them and say:

"Blessed be thy feet that have brought thee in these ways." (He kisses her feet.)

"Blessed be thy knees that shall kneel at the sacred altar." (He kisses her knees.)

"Blessed be thy womb, without which we would not be." (He kisses her Organ of Generation.)

"Blessed by thy breasts, formed in beauty and in strength." (He kisses her breasts.)

"Blessed be thy lips, which shall utter the sacred names." (He kisses her lips.)

Take measure thus: height, around forehead, across the heart, and across the genitals. Magus says, "Be pleased to kneel," and helps her kneel before the altar. He ties the end of the Cable Tow to a ring in the altar, so that the postulant is bent sharply forward, with her head almost touching the floor. He also ties her feet together with the short cord. Magus strikes three knells on the bell and says, "Art ready to swear that thou wilt always be true to the Art?"

Witch: "I am."

Magus strikes seven knells on the bell and says, "Before ye are sworn, art willing to pass the ordeal and be purified?"

Witch: "I am."

Magus strikes eleven knells on the bell, takes the scourge from the altar, and gives a series of three, seven, nine, and 21 strokes with the scourge across the postulant's buttocks. Magus says, "Ye have bravely passed the test. Art always ready to help, protect, and defend thy Brothers and Sisters of the Art?"

Witch: "I am."

Magus: "Art armed?"

Witch: "With a knife in my hair."

Magus: "Then on that knife wilt thou swear absolute secrecy?"

Witch: "I will."

Magus: "Then say after me. 'I, (name), in the presence of the Mighty Ones, do of my own will and accord, most solemnly swear that I will ever keep secret and never reveal the secrets of the Art, except it be to a proper person, properly prepared, within a circle such as I am now in. All this I swear by my hopes of a future life, mindful that my measure has been taken, and may my weapons turn against me if I break this my solemn oath.'"

Magus now unbinds her feet, unties the Cable Tow from the altar, removes the blindfold, and helps her up to her feet.

Magus says, "I hereby sign thee with the triple sign.

"I consecrate thee with oil." (He anoints her with oil on the womb, the right breast, the left breast, and the womb again.)

"I consecrate thee with wine." (He anoints her with wine in the same pattern.)

"I consecrate thee with my lips" (he kisses her in the same pattern), "Priestess and Witch."

Magus now unbinds her hands and removes the last cord, saying, "Now I Present to thee the Working Tools of a Witch. "First the Magic Sword. With this, as with the Athame, thou canst form all Magic Circles, dominate, subdue, and punish all rebellious Spirits and Demons, and even persuade the Angels and Geniuses. With this in your hand you are the ruler of the Circle.

"Next I present the Athame. This is the true Witch's weapon and has all the powers of the Magic Sword .

"Next I present the White-Handled Knife. Its use is to form all instruments used in the Art. It can only be properly used within a Magic Circle .

"Next I present the Wand. Its use is to call up and control certain Angels and geniuses, to whom it would not be mete to use the Magic Sword .

"Next I present the pentacles. These are for the purpose of calling up appropriate Spirits .

"Next I present the Censer of Incense. This is used to encourage and welcome Good Spirits and to banish Evil Spirits.

"Next I present the scourge. This is a sign of power and domination. It is also to cause suffering and purification, for it is written, to learn you must suffer and be purified. Art willing to suffer to learn?"

Witch: "I am."

Magus: "Next, and lastly I present the Cords. They are of use to bind the sigils in the Art, the material basis, and to enforce thy will. Also they are necessary in the oath. I Salute thee in the name of Aradia and Cernunnos, Newly made Priestess and Witch." Magus strikes seven knells on the bell and kisses Witch again, then circumambulates with her, proclaiming to the four quarters, "Hear, ye Mighty Ones, (name) hath been consecrated Priestess and Witch of the Gods." (Note, if ceremony ends here, close circle with "I thank ye for attending, and I dismiss ye to your pleasant abodes. Hail and farewell." If not, go to next degree.)'[107]

Initiation: Second Degree

<u>Magus binds Witch as before, but does not blindfold her, and circumambulates with her, proclaims to the four quarters,</u> "Hear, ye Mighty Ones, (name), a duly consecrated Priestess and Witch, is now properly prepared to be made a High Priestess and Witch Queen." Magus now leads her thrice around the circle with the half-running, half-dancing step, halts south of the altar, has the Witch kneel, and ties her down to the altar as before.

Magus: "To attain this sublime degree, it is necessary to suffer and be purified. Art ready to suffer to Learn?"

Priestess Witch: "I am."

Magus: "I prepare thee to take the great oath."

He strikes three knells on the bell, and again gives the series of three, seven, nine, and 21 strokes with the scourge as before.

Magus: "I now give thee a new name: _____.

<u>Magus: "Repeat thy new name after me, I, (name), swear</u> upon my mother's womb and by mine Honor among men and among my brothers and sisters of the Art<u>, that I will never reveal to any at all</u>

---

[107] The Gardnerian Book of Shadows, by Gerald Gardner, at sacred-texts.com

any of the secrets of the Art, except it be to a worthy person, properly prepared, in the center of a Magic Circle, such as I am now in. This I swear by my hopes of Salvation, my past lives, and my hopes of future ones to come, and I devote myself to utter destruction if I break this my solemn oath."

Magus kneels, placing left hand under her knees and right hand on her head, thus forming magic link.

Magus: "I hereby will all my power into you." Wills.

Magus now unties her feet, unties the Cable Tow from the altar, and helps the Witch to her feet.

Magus: "I hereby sign and consecrate you with the great Magic Sign. Remember how it is formed and you will always recognize it.

"I consecrate thee with oil." (He anoints her with oil on her womb, right breast, left hip, right hip, left breast, and womb again, thus tracing a point-down pentacle.)

"I consecrate thee with wine." (He anoints her with wine in the same pattern.)

"I consecrate thee with my lips" (he kisses her in the same pattern), "High Priestess and Witch Queen."

Magus now unbinds Witch's hands and removes the cord, saying, "Newly made High Priestess and Witch Queen" "you will now use the working tools in turn.

First, the Magic Sword; with it you will scribe the Magic Circle

"Secondly, the Athame" (Form Circle)

"Thirdly, the White Handled Knife" (use)

"Fourthly, the Wand" (Wave to 4 Quarters)

"Fifthly, the Pentacle" (Show to 4 Quarters)

"Sixthly, the Censer of Incense" (Circle, cense)

"Seventhly, the cords; bind me as I bound you." Witch binds Magus and ties him to Altar.

Magus: "Learn, in Witchcraft, thou must ever return triple. As I scourged thee, so thou must scourge me, but triple. So where you received 3, return 9; where you received 7, return 21; where you received 9, return 27; where you received 21, return 63." Witch scourges Magus as instructed, 120 strokes total.

Magus: "Thou hast obeyed the Law. But mark well, when thou receivest good, so equally art bound to return good threefold."

Witch now unbinds Magus and helps him to his feet. Magus, taking the new Initiate by the hand and holding the Athame in the other, passes once round the Circle, proclaiming at the Four Quarters, "Hear, Ye Mighty Ones, (name) hath been duly consecrated High

Priestess and Witch Queen." (Note, if ceremony ends here, close circle with "Hail and farewell." If not go to next degree.) [108]

Initiation: Third Degree

Magus: "Ere we proceed with this sublime degree, I must beg purification at thy hands."

High Priestess binds Magus and ties him down to the altar. She circumambulates three times, and scourges Magus with three, seven, nine, and 21 strokes. She then unbinds him and helps him to his feet. Magus now binds the High Priestess and ties her down to the altar. <u>He circumambulates, proclaiming to the four quarters</u>, "Hear, ye mighty Ones, the twice consecrate and Holy (name), High Priestess and Witch Queen, <u>is properly prepared</u> and will now proceed to erect the Sacred Altar." Magus scourges High Priestess with three, seven, nine, and 21 strokes. Cakes and wine may now be taken.

Magus: "Now I must reveal to you a great Mystery."

Note: if High Priestess has performed this rite before, omit these words. High Priestess assumes Osiris position.

---

[108] The Gardnerian Book of Shadows, by Gerald Gardner, at sacred-texts.com

Magus: "Assist me to erect the Ancient Altar, at which in days past all worshipped, the Great Altar of all things. For in the old times a woman was the Altar. Thus was the altar made and so placed [Priestess lies down in such a way that her vagina is approximately at the centre of the circle], and the sacred place was the point within the centre of the circle, as we of old times have been taught, that the point within the <u>centre</u> is the origin of all things. Therefore should we adore it."

"Therefore, whom we adore, we also invoke, by the power of the lifted lance." Invokes. "O circle of stars , whereof our Father is but the younger brother , "Marvel beyond imagination, soul of infinite space, before whom time is ashamed, the mind bewildered and understanding dark, not unto thee may we attain unless thine image be of love .

"Therefore, by seed and root, and stem and bud and leaf and flower and fruit do we invoke thee, O, Queen of space, O dew of light, O continuous one of the Heavens . "Let it be ever thus, that men speak not of Thee as one, but as none, and let them not speak of thee at all, since thou art continuous, for thou art the point within the circle , which we adore , the fount of life without which we would not be . <u>"And in this way truly are erected the Holy Twin Pillars Boaz and Joachim [kisses breasts]. In beauty and strength were they erected, to the wonder and glory of all men."</u>

(Eightfold Kiss: 3 points, Lips, 2 Breasts and back to lips; 5 points)

"O Secrets of secrets that art hidden in the being of all lives. Not thee do we adore, for that which adoreth is also thou. Thou art that and That am I.

"I am the flame that burns in every man, and in the core of every star.

"I am Life and the giver of Life, yet therefore is the knowledge of me the Knowledge of Death.

"I am alone, the Lord within ourselves whose name is Mystery of Mysteries.

"Make open the path of intelligence between us. For these truly are the 5 points of fellowship feet to feet, knee to knee, groin to groin, breast to breast, arms around back, lips to lips, by the Great and Holy Names Abracadabra, Aradia, and Cernunnos.

Magus and High Priestess: "Encourage our hearts, Let thy Light crystallize itself in our blood, fulfilling us of Resurrection, for there is no part of us that is not of the Gods."

(Exchange Names.)

Closing the Circle High Priestess Circumambulates, proclaiming, "The twice consecrate High Priestess greets ye Mighty Ones, and dismisseth ye to your pleasant abodes. Hail and Farewell."

She draws the banishing pentacle at each quarter.[109]

Quasi Freemasonry in Wicca

In the above examples we have covered the direct influences of Freemasonry on Wicca, however there additional indirect influences of Freemasonry on Wicca too. These influences are best seen in how material from the Quasi Masonic organisation the OTO have helped the development of Wicca.

There has been a great deal written about working with the moon in the last 50 years by modern pagans, its central role in neo-paganism and 20th century religion Wicca is well documented by a number of books on the subject. The technique of drawing down the moon is a major part of Wicca, as this is an introductory notes it is prudent to cover this first. There are several different versions of this method in Wicca, one adaptation of the approach from Gardnerian Book of Shadows in brief is:

'The High Priestess stands in front of Altar which is in the North and faces south. She stands in Goddess position (arms crossed as Osiris). High Priest/Magus, kneels in front of her and draws a pentacle on her body with a Phallus-headed Wand, and invokes, I Invoke and beseech Thee, O mighty Mother of all life and fertility. By seed and root, by stem and bud, by leaf and flower and fruit, by Life and Love, do I invoke Thee to descend into the body of thy servant and High Priestess [name]. The Moon having been drawn

---

[109] The Gardnerian Book of Shadows, by Gerald Gardner, at sacred-texts.com

down, i.e., link established, Magus and other men give Fivefold Kiss:

(kissing feet) Blessed be thy feet, that have brought thee in these ways;

(kissing knees) Blessed be thy knees, that shall kneel at the sacred altar;

(kissing womb) Blessed be thy womb, without which we would not be;

(kissing breasts) Blessed be thy breasts, formed in beauty and in strength;

(kissing lips) Blessed be thy lips, that shall speak the sacred names. Women all bow.

If there be an initiation, then at this time the High Priest/ Magus and the High Priestess in Goddess position (Arms Crossed) says the Charge while the Initiate stands outside the circle.'[110]

Next the Charge of the Goddess is recited:

'Magus/High Priest: Listen to the words of the Great mother, who was of old also called among men, Artemis, Astarte, Anahita,

---

[110] *Drawing Down the Moon,* The Gardnerian Book of Shadows, by Gerald Gardner.

Dione, Melusine, Aphrodite, Cerridwen, Diana, Arianrhod, Bride, (insert your preferred goddesses here) and by many other names.

High Priestess: At mine Altars the youth of Lacedaemon in Sparta made due sacrifice. Whenever ye have need of anything, once in the month, and better it be when the moon is full. Then ye shall assemble in some secret place and adore the spirit of Me who am Queen of all Witcheries. There ye shall assemble, ye who are fain to learn all sorcery, yet who have not won its deepest secrets. To these will I teach things that are yet unknown. And ye shall be free from slavery, and as a sign that ye be really free, ye shall be naked in your rites, and ye shall dance, sing, feast, make music, and love, all in my praise. For mine is the ecstasy of the Spirit, and mine is also joy on earth. For my Law is Love unto all beings. Keep pure your highest ideals. Strive ever towards it. Let naught stop you or turn you aside. For mine is the secret which opens upon the door of youth; and mine is the cup of the Wine of Life: and the Cauldron of Cerridwen, which is the Holy Grail of Immortality. I am the Gracious Goddess who gives the gift of Joy unto the heart of Man. Upon Earth I give the knowledge of the Spirit Eternal, and beyond death I give peace and freedom, and reunion with those who have gone before. Nor do I demand aught in sacrifice, for behold, I am the Mother of all things, and my love is poured out upon earth.

Magus/High Priest: Hear ye the words of the Star Goddess, She in the dust of whose feet are the hosts of Heaven, whose body encircleth the universe.

High Priestess: I who am the beauty of the green earth; and the White Moon amongst the Stars; and the mystery of the Waters; and the desire of the heart of man. I call unto thy soul: arise and come unto me. For I am the Soul of nature who giveth life to the Universe; From me all things proceed; and unto me, all things must return. Beloved of the Gods and men, thine inmost divine self shall be enfolded in the raptures of the infinite. Let my worship be within the heart that rejoiceth, for behold: all acts of love and pleasure are my rituals; and therefore let there be Beauty and Strength, Power and Compassion, Honor and Humility, Mirth and reverence within you. And thou who thinkest to seek me, know that thy seeking and yearning shall avail thee not unless thou know the mystery, that if that which thou seekest thou findest not within thee, thou wilt never find it without thee, for behold; I have been with thee from the beginning, and I am that which is attained at the end of desire.'[111]

In this Wiccan method which uses male / female polarity, the High Priest draws down the moon onto the High Priestess, who then

---

[111] *The Charge,* The Gardnerian Book of Shadows, by Gerald Gardner.

gives voice to the Moon Goddess. During the Charge of the Goddesses, in a way a plethora of goddesses are being channelled through the priestess, not just the moon, the moon acts as the starting point, and the initial focus. The priestess following from being the Moon Goddess, then channels the Earth Goddess too, the Great Mother. The next stage is clearly marked by High Priest/Magus saying:

'Hear ye the words of the Star Goddess, She in the dust of whose feet are the hosts of Heaven, whose body encircleth the universe.'

The High Priestess now channels the Star Goddess, in her myriad of forms, for example the Egyptian star goddess Nuit. This is perhaps the climax of the oracle, giving voice to star goddess Nuit. How can we be certain it is the Egyptian star goddess Nuit? The answer lies in those parts of the Wiccan drawing down the moon and 'Charge of the Goddess' that appear to be based partly on the Gnostic Mass and Book of the Law by Aleister Crowley. Specifically in the section in the Ceremony of the Opening of the Veil in the Gnostic Mass reads:

The Priest:

O circle of Stars whereof our Father is but the younger brother, marvel beyond imagination, soul of infinite space, before whom Time is Ashamed, the mind bewildered, and the understanding dark, not unto Thee may we attain, unless Thine image be Love.

Therefore by seed and root and stem and bud and leaf and flower and fruit do we invoke Thee.[112]

Further more in Book of the Law (Liber AL vel Legis) line 27 reads: 'Then the priest answered & said unto the Queen of Space, kissing her lovely brows, and the dew of her light bathing his whole body in a sweet-smelling perfume of sweat: O Nuit, continuous one of Heaven, let it be ever thus; that men speak not of Thee as One but as None; and let them speak not of thee at all, since thou art continuous!'

It is perhaps appropriate to finish this work by the most moving lines of chapter 1 of *Liber AL* and it should also be examined here, starting from line 61 reads:

'But to love me is better than all things; if under the night-stars in the desert thou presently burnest mine incense before me, invoking me with a pure heart, and the serpent flame therein, thou shalt come a little to lie in my bosom. For one kiss wilt thou then be willing to give all; but whoso gives one particle of dust shall lose all in that hour. Ye shall gather goods and store of women and spices; ye shall wear rich jewels; ye shall exceed the nations of the earth in splendour and pride; but always in the love of me, and so shall ye come to my joy. I charge you earnestly to come before me in a single robe, and covered with a rich head-dress. I love you! I yearn to you! Pale or purple, veiled or voluptuous, I who am all pleasure and purple, and drunkenness of the innermost sense, desire you.

---

[112] *Liber XV* The Gnostic Mass by Aliester Crowley.

Put on the wings, and arouse the coiled splendour within you: come unto me! To me! To me! Sing the raptuous love-song unto me! Burn to me perfumes! Wear to me jewels! Drink to me, for I love you! I love you. I am the blue-lidded daughter of sunset; I am the naked brilliance of the voluptuous night-sky. To me! To me!!"[113]

Conclusions

In the above examples we have covered the direct influences of Freemasonry on Wicca, however there are additional indirect influences of Freemasonry on Wicca too. These influences are best seen in how material from the Quasi-Masonic organisation OTO have helped development of Wicca.

In this essay a multitude of links between Freemasonry and Wicca were demonstrated in the form of ritual materials, and, the number of key players in Wicca and Neo-Pagan revival who were Freemasons or had close links with Freemasonry. The perception of the general decline of interest in Freemasonry should be re-examined in this light, while Freemasonry might be on a decline in the last few decades, its decedents are on an incline. This implies a greater number of people are aligned to ideals of Freemasonry than it may appear at first, the social and anthropological impact of this should be borne in mind.

---

[113] *Liber AL vel Legis* by Aliester Crowley.

Acknowledgments:

I would like to thanks Hannah Fox and Graham King at the Witchcraft Museum, Boscastle, Cornwall for their help with material shown in figure 18 and figure 19.

I would like to thank Mogg Morgan of Oxford Golden Dawn Occult Society, and Jack Daw for their helpful comments.

I would like to thank Sacred Texts (sacred-texts.com) for making their resources available.

Bibliography and Further reading:

Barrett, David V. *The Atlas of Secret Societies*, Octopus Publishing Group, 2008.

Bogdan, Henrik, *Western esotericism and rituals of initiation*, State University of New York Press, 2007.

Booth, Martin, A Magick Life: a biography of Aleister Crowley, Coronet Books, 2000.

Bott, Adrian, *The Great Wicca Hoax - Part I*, White Dragon Magazine, Lughnasa 2001.

Bott, Adrian, *The Great Wicca Hoax II: Attack of the Crones,* White Dragon Magazine, Lughnasa 2002.

Buchanan-Brown, John and Chevalier, Jean and Gheerbrant, Alain, *The Penguin Dictionary of Symbols*, Penguin Books Ltd, 1996.

Carr-Gomm, Philip, *Druid Renaissance,* Thorsons, 1998.

Churton, Tobias, *The Magus of Freemasonry: The Mysterious Life of Elias Ashmole - Scientist, Alchemist and Founder of the Royal Society,* Inner Traditions Bear and Company, 2006.

Cotterell, Arthur, *The Ultimate Encyclopedia of Mythology,* Hermes House, 2003.

Crowley, Aleister, *Magick in Theory and Practice,* Red Wheel/Weiser, 1994.

Crowley, Aleister, *Liber XV* 'The Gnostic Mass', *Liber AL vel Legis,* Liber DCCCXIII vel ARARITA, sacred-texts.com

Crowley, Aleister, Symonds, John, Grant, Kenneth, *The Confessions of Aleister Crowley : An Autohagiography,* Arkana; New edition , 1989.

Farrar, Janet and Stewart, *The Witches Way,* Hale, 1984.

Gardner, Gerald, *The Gardnerian Book of Shadows,* sacred-texts.com

Heselton, Philip, *Wiccan Roots,* Cappall Bann, 2000.

Howard, Michael, *Modern Wicca: A History From Gerald Gardner to the Present,* Llewellyn, 2010.

Hutton, Ronald, *The Triumph of the Moon: A History of Modern Pagan Witchcraft,* Oxford University Press, 1999.

Hutton, Ronald, *Witches, Druids and King Arthur,* Hambledon Continuum, 2003.

Hutton, Ronald, *The Druids: A History,* Hambledon Continuum, 2008.

Kelly, Adrian, *Crafting the Art of Magic,* Book I A History of Modern Witchcraft, 1939-1964, Llewellyn, 1991.

Jordan, Michael, *Witches-an encyclopaedia of paganism and magic*, Kyle Cathie Ltd, 1996.

Lamond, Frederic, *Fifty Years of Wicca*, Green Magic, 2004.

Lomas, Robert, *Turning the Hiram Key: Making Darkness Visible*, Lewis Masonic, 2007 edition.

Lomas, Robert, *The Secret Science of Masonic Initiation*, Lewis Masonic, 2008.

Liddel, WE. and Howard, Michael *Pickingill Papers the Origins of the Gardnerian Craft*, Capall Bann, 1994.

Morgan, Path, *The Secrets of the Freemasons*, Arcturus, 2006.

Nurbakhsh Dr.J.*Great Satan Eblis*, Khaniqah Nimatullahi Publications, (1986).

Rankine, David; D'Este, Sorita, *Wicca Magical Beginnings*, Avalonia, 2008.

Shah, Idries, *The Sufis*, Jonathan Cape, 1971.

Zarcone, Thierry Professor. *Gnostic/Sufi Symbols and Ideas In Turkish & Persian Freemasonry and in Masonic-Inspired Organisations*, the Canterbury papers vol5, Knowledge of the heart: Gnostic Movements and Secret Traditions, Lewis Masonic, 2006.

Sacred Plants (Drugs in religion)

This was written in 1993, it has been slightly updated for this collection.

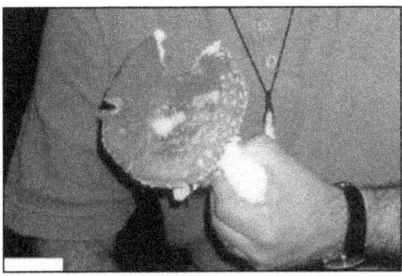

Figure 22: Fly Agarics mushroom

Since the dawn of time mankind has asked himself about his origins and the existence of God and has looked for ways to make connections with the godhead and the divine. The ancient religions and their customs and approaches to reach this aim have now become less popular due to the view of the established monotheistic religions. In these ancient religions the whole question of using drugs in religious ceremonies is looked at from a different angle to the modern times. The majority of today's main religions of the world are monotheistic and have a limited belief in the 'spiritual realm', and 'officially' dismiss the use of drugs for religious purposes. However, even after 3000 years of monotheistic prophets trying to close the pharmakon, this back door to god's house is still used by some, even though god might ask you to go out of his house and use the front door like everyone else!

This essay aims to look at the magical practices that have been carried out for hundreds of years, and will try to explain the pharmacological reasons behind the experiences of the practitioners who were mainly of high social status in their communities. They were priests, shamans and wise people, whose advice was taken by the rulers; hence effecting the lives of many people, and setting the basis for many religious belief patterns.[114]

The use of drugs for religious purposes is probably as old as man himself. For example, in ancient Greece people under the influence of Henbane were known to become prophetic, and the Priestesses of the Delphic Oracle claimed to have inhaled the smoke from smouldering Henbane. In Roman, times wine adulterated with Deadly Nightshade was used during the Bacchanalian orgies.

The use of plants for witchcraft and sorcery was widespread in the middle ages in Europe. In the New World, the Aztec priests used Ololiuqui, Teonaucalt and Peyolt in their ceremonies. Even to this day in Mexico Shamans and witch doctors play a vital role in the daily life of the local population, with their visions, prescriptions and medicine. One might imagine that such practices should no longer be acceptable to people in central and south America;

---

[114] Disclaimer: This chapter is intended as an informational guide only. Due caution should be taken by the reader should they decide to use any of the substances mentioned in some of the texts herein. The author and publisher cannot take responsibility for any allergic reaction or any other negative results.

nations which have been turning to Christianity for the last four hundred years, and where the Catholic church has a firm foothold.

The magico-religious practices of the Aztecs are still widespread, but not as they offer a better philosophical explanation of life and the world, but because the hallucinogenic drugs which are used can alter the consciousness to such a degree that the users gain a religious experience. Interestingly, some incantations recited today are the same one which has been intoned for thousands of years. However, they now invoke the names of the Virgin Mary, St Peter, and St Paul. This process of combing pre-Christian religious practices with Christian beliefs is called dual observance, and can be seen both in the New World and Europe. It seems the drugs and chants are the main consistent components in these religious rites, and not the names of the spirits of old, or Saints of the new religion or recitations from the Bible.

The following plants and brews have played a major role in the history of magic: Deadly Nightshade, Henbane, Mandrake Datura, Brugsmansie, Ololiuqui, Teonnacacatl, Peyolt, and Ayahuasca. Here, each one will be briefly discussed and their major properties highlighted.

The methods of administration of these plants (drugs) are varied, but mainly the plants are mixed with oils, hence they penetrate through the skin or are absorbed via the sweat glands. This allows the psychoactive tropane allkaloids (e.g. hyosciene) to reach the blood stream and brain without passing directly into the gastrointestinal (GI) tract and cause poisoning.

Datura and Brugsmansie

The chemical hyoscine (Scopolamine) is a major constituent of many plant species of Datura and plants of related genus Brugmansa, it has both medicinal and hallucinogenic uses.

Hyoscine is classified as an antimuscarinic or muscarinic blocking drugs as it competitively blocks the action of acetylcholine at both the central and peripheral muscarinic receptors, (for both M1 and M2 receptors). Apart from acetylcholine other antagonists for M1 and M2 receptor subtypes are muscarine and cabamycholine. This drug suppresses REM sleep and on withdrawal dream recall and nightmares are increased.

The Native American tribes used this drug for its magical hallucinogenic property, combined with many other factors for its maximum effect, this includes using chants, the rhythmic beating of drums and prolonged dances, which in some cases went on for several days. After that the participants collapsed from exhaustion and saw visions of many spiritual beings. The physiological and psychological changes that take place in the human body and mind during Native American rites are of great interest, even when no drugs were used. It seems that some Shaman of higher rank were able to go into a trance and make prophecies without the use of any drugs, and, solely relies on the ritual dances to reach the trance state. This is a subject of study for psychologists regarding the effects of folklore on the 'primitive mind' (the type of study that makes the 'natives restless', as nothing is more annoying than a person in a suit and tie taking notes during your 'secret' religious ceremony).

To summerise the uses of the drug Hyoscine, which is a constituent part of Datura (Thorn Apple) and the Brugmansia plant:

· Various witches brews

· Causing a death-like sleep

· Flying Ointment

· For transformation into an animal form

· Used for communication with dead ancestors

· In Africa for trials by ordeal and complex puberty rites involving flagellation and ceremonial deflowering

The medical properties of Hyoscine include:

· Treatment for fever

· Used for mental disorders

· A treatment for heart disease

· A cure for Pneumonia

The use of Hyoscine has been continued to the present times, Eg. NASA has Hyoscine plasters as a treatment for motion sickness which can be experienced during space travel.

Ololiqui and Teonanacatl

Ololiqui was used by the Aztecs as a magical brew for divination, and sacrificial ceremonies. It was prepared from the seeds of the Morning Glory plant, Rivera Corymbosa. These seeds seem to contain Lysergic acid amides with similar structure to Lysergic Acid Dietylamide (LSD). However, it is about twenty times less potent than LSD, the origins of hallucinogenic effects experienced by the Aztecs are explained therefore. Lysergic Acid amides act at certain serotonin receptors on the neurones in the mid brain. In small doses LSD is a serotonin mimic, but in larger doses it antagonises the effects of a neurotransmitter. These serotonin dependent neurones connect with other noradrenalin dependent neurones that are intimately involved in the regulation of behavioural responses to sensory stimulation. Hence during a trip, sensory disorientation occurs, also increased blood pressure, sweating, rapid breathing and palpitations of the heart, mood swings, great fear or manic excitement, which are similar to the schizophrenic state.

Teonanacatl mushrooms and its mushroom cult has survived for three thousand years due to its ability when the participants get intoxicated a series of unearthly experiences occur. Today in Mexico, Mazutec Indians have complex rituals for the collection and consumptions of mushrooms. The main psychotic constituents are psilocybin and small amounts of Psilocin (similar to serotonin) which have 1% potency of LSD.

The Peyote religion has a following of quarter of million people in North America (i.e. the Native American Church). This church uses the peyote cactus, which is widespread in Mexico, it has a greenish grey crown atop 'a parsnip-like root. the crown is sliced from root and dried to form mescal buttons'[115]. This can be obtained legally via mail order catalogues in North America. Mescaline is the major component of peyote, however, it has only 0.2% of the hallucinogenic potency of LSD. Supposedly it has the added advantage of one doesn't get any 'bad trips'. This of course is the basis of designer drugs such as DOM and MDNA (Ecstasy). Peyote hunts are carried out as part of religious practices of the Huichol Indians of Mexico, during which the shaman lead pilgrims to collect peyote. The mescaline in peyote gives visual hallucinations and distortion of time and space.

Ayahuasca

Finally the plant Ayahuasca (caapi) is also widely used for the purposes of divination and prophesy by Native Americans. The brew is made by boiling the bark and consuming it before ceremonies are performed. The result can be coloured visions which may occur the during the ceremony.

---

[115] Murder, Magic, and Medicine by J. Mann (Oxford University Press, 1992).

Some of the Native American tribes in the Amazon basin have a ceremony for showing the animal spirit of a person to him. During the ceremony the subject falls sleep and sees himself transformed into an animal which is very closely resembles the main characteristics of that person; for example the hunters tend to have spirits such as Jaguars or birds of prey. One suspect Caapi was used in the brew which was consumed in these rites. Interestingly, when harmine and harmaline (main constituents of caapi) are taken under controlled conditions in the lab by 'western' experimenters who here had no exposure to Amazons Indian myth cycles, they too had similar visions as the Amazon Indian shamans. This could be interpreted as the plant triggering specific brain pathways and hence the result was the same no matter who took it, or maybe the plant is the 'key' for unlocking a specific 'door' to a particular deity!

Harmine and Harmaline block serotonin receptors in the brain (cross reactive with LSD and psilocybin), also they inhibit the oxidative metabolism of the other brain amines, hence complete disturbance of the Central Nervous System (CNS). They have a further property which is to cause sexual excitation, hence it was used in initiation rites for adolescent boys in the Amazon basin and the ceremonies often included other stimulatory acts such as flagellation!

Homa or Soma

Homa is the name of a legendary plant with medicinal and spiritual properties that is mentioned in ancient texts from both India and Persia. Actually, it is the name of the deity or spirit presiding over the Homa plant, as the spirit was seen as a deity in its own right (see Zoroastrian Hymn to Homa)[116], Homa (Sanskrit Soma), is lord of the harvests. Poets, warriors, and priests drank of it. Its juices flowed yellow as the rays of the sun, liquid as the life-giving rain; the drink extracted from the Homa plant had qualities more divine by far than these. It gave bravery to warriors in battle, and visions to priests. No one knows for sure what Homa was—some suggest it was hemp based—but Zoroastrians seem to have used an ephedrine for a similar purpose. Drinking Homa resulted in a trancelike state.

Also, it is said Homa was stirred together with the fat of a bull to make the drink of immortality. Some academics have suggested another possible candidate for Homa might have been the fly agaric mushroom (*Amanita muscaria*), though the majority believe that *Ephedra* was used in the making of the Homa. According to *The Encyclopedia of Psychoactive Plants* by Christian Rätsch, some traces of the Homa cult still remain in Iran today, where the drink is said to be brewed either from pomegranate juice (*Punica granatum L.*) and ephedra (*Ephedra spp*) or from rue (*Ruta graveolens L*) and milk. Some,

---

[116] http://www.avesta.org/yasna/y9to11s.htm

basing their theories on the Zoroastrian creation story of the white Bull being slayed by Ahriman, have suggested that the Bull is Homa and perhaps the later slaying of the Bull by Mithras is a symbol of the pressing of Homa juice! This is a controversial but interesting view, as Ahura Mazda feeds the white Bull hemp to sedate him so when Ahriman kills him, the Bull wouldn't feel the pain. From the Bull comes all life —both animals and plants.[117]

The drink based on Homa (Soma) is lost to us, for modern Magi a good alternative could be milk with honey mixed in (land of Ambrosia). Also wine, or mead, if one prefer something with alcohol, or perhaps like the Eleusinian mysteries water with grain soaked in it.

The Homa Yasht (Yasna 10) tells us about the plant's properties, espically section 4 to 8:

'1. Let the Demon-gods and Goddesses fly far away 1 from hence, and let the good Sraosha make here his home! [And may the good Blessedness here likewise dwell], and may she here spread delight and peace within this house, Ahura's, which is sanctified by Homa, bringing righteousness (to all).

---

[117] The Encyclopedia of Psychoactive Plants: Ethnopharmacology and Its Applications by Christian Rätsch, John R. Baker, trans. (Rochester, Vt.: Park Street Press, 2004), 747–48.

2. At the first force of thy pressure, O intelligent! I praise thee with my voice, while I grasp at first thy shoots. At thy next pressure, O intelligent! I praise thee with my voice, when as with full force of a man I crush thee down.

3. I praise the cloud that waters thee, and the rains which make thee grow on the summits of the mountains; and I praise thy lofty mountains where the Homa branches spread.

4. This wide earth do I praise, expanded far (with paths), the productive, the full bearing, thy mother, holy plant! Yea, I praise the lands where thou dost grow, sweet-scented, swiftly spreading, the good growth of the Lord. O Homa, thou growest on the mountains, apart on many paths, and there still may'st thou flourish. The springs of Righteousness most verily thou art, (and the fountains of the ritual find their source in thee)!

5. Grow (then) because I pray to thee on all thy stems and branches, in all thy shoots (and tendrils) increase thou through my word!

6. Homa grows while he is praised, and the man who praises him is therewith more victorious. The lightest pressure of thee, Homa, thy feeblest praise, the slightest tasting of thy juice, avails to the thousand-smiting of the Daevas.

7. Wasting doth vanish from that house, and with it foulness, whither in verity they bear thee, and where thy praise in truth is sung, the drink of Homa, famed, health-bringing (as thou art). [(Pâzand) to his village and abode they bear him.]

8. All other toxicants go hand in hand with Rapine of the bloody spear, but Homa's stirring power goes hand in hand with friendship. [Light is the drunkenness of Homa (Pâzand).]

Who as a tender son caresses Homa, forth to the bodies of such persons Homa comes to heal.

9. Of all the healing virtues, Homa, whereby thou art a healer, grant me some. Of all the victorious powers, whereby thou art a victor, grant me some. A faithful praiser will I be to thee, O Homa, and a faithful praiser (is) a better (thing) than Righteousness the Best; so hath the Lord, declaring (it), decreed.

10. Swift and wise hath the well-skilled 2 Deity created thee; swift and wise on high Haraiti did He, the well-skilled, plant thee.

11. And taught (by implanted instinct) on everyside, the bounteous birds have carried thee to the Peaks-above-the-eagles, to the

mount's extremest summit, to the gorges and abysses, to the heights of many pathways, to the snow-peaks ever whitened.

12. There, Homa, on the ranges dost thou grow of many kinds. Now thou growest of milky whiteness, and now thou growest golden; and forth thine healing liquors flow for the inspiring of the pious. So terrify away from me the (death's) aim of the curser. So terrify and crush his thought who stands as my maligner.

13. Praise be to thee, O Homa, (for he makes the poor man's thoughts as great as any of the richest whomsoever.) Praise be to Homa, (for he makes the poor man's thoughts as great as when mind reacheth culmination.) With manifold retainers dost thou, O Homa, endow the man who drinks thee mixed with milk; yea, more prosperous thou makest him, and more endowed with mind.

14. Do not vanish from me suddenly like milk-drops in the rain; let thine exhilarations go forth ever vigorous and fresh; and let them come to me with strong effect. Before thee, holy Homa, thou bearer of the ritual truth, and around thee would I cast this body, a body which (as all) may see (is fit for gift and) grown.

15. I renounce with vehemence the murderous woman's emptiness, the Gaini's, hers, with intellect dethroned 1. She vainly thinks to foil us, and would beguile both Fire-priest and Homa; but she herself,

deceived therein, shall perish. And when she sits at home, and wrongly eats of Homa's offering, priest's mother will that never make her, nor give her holy sons!

16. To five do I belong, to five others do I not; of the good thought am I, of the evil am I not; of the good word am I, of the evil am I not; of the good deed am I, and of the evil, not. To Obedience am I given, and to deaf disobedience, not; to the saint do I belong, and to the wicked, not; and so from this on till the ending shall be the spirits' parting. (The two shall here divide.)

17. Thereupon spake Zarathustra: Praise to Homa, Mazda-made. Good is Homa, Mazda-made. All the plants of Homa praise I, on the heights of lofty mountains, in the gorges of the valleys, in the clefts (of sundered hill-sides) cut for the bundles bound by women. From the silver cup I pour Thee to the golden chalice over. Let me not thy (sacred) liquor spill to earth, of precious cost.

18. These are thy Gâthas, holy Homa, these thy songs, and these thy teachings 1, and these thy truthful ritual words, health imparting, victory-giving, from harmful hatred healing giving.

19. These and thou art mine, and forth let thine exhilarations flow; bright and sparkling let them hold on their (steadfast) way; for light are thine exhilaration(s), and flying lightly come they here. Victory-

giving smiteth Homa, victory-giving is it worshipped; with this Gâthic word we praise it.

20. Praise to the Kine; praise and victory (be) spoken to her! Food for the Kine, and pasture! 'For the Kine let thrift use toil; yield thou us food 3.'

21. We worship the yellow lofty one; we worship Homa who causes progress, who makes the settlements advance; we worship Homa who drives death afar; yea, we worship all the Homa plants. And we worship (their) blessedness, and the Fravashi of Zarathustra Spitâma, the saint.' [118]

There is no doubt that hallucinogenic drugs have contributed a great deal to the way ancient cultures organised their way of life and their religious beliefs. Without these drugs, non of the pagan religions would have lasted as long as they have and still be practised in parts of the world; the strange experiences of priestess and great visions of shamans we could say largely are a result of taking hallucinogenic drugs. But, we can't fully prove this; history has taught us that no idea or belief survives for long unless there is some element of truth in it. The question of recreational verses the sacred use of magical plants has kept many magical practitioners busy. Does the over use of drugs at nightclubs devalue them as

---

[118] http://www.avesta.org/yasna/y9to11s.htm and http://www.sacred-texts.com/zor/sbe31/sbe31032.htm

sacred tools for altering reality? Is it respectful to spirit of plant to use them for non-religious purposes without paying respect to them?

Bibliography and Further reading

Murder, Magic, and Medicine by J. Mann (Oxford University Press, 1992).

Biochemistry (The Benjamin/Cummings series in life sciences and chemistry) by C.K. Mathews, K.E.Van Holde, K.F. van Holde, (Benjamin-Cummings Publishing Company, 1990).

Pharmakon: Drugs and the Imagination, by Julian Vayne, (Mandrake of Oxford, 2006).

The Encyclopedia of Psychoactive Plants: Ethnopharmacology and Its Applications by Christian Rätsch, John R. Baker, trans. (Rochester, Vt.: Park Street Press, 2004).

The Right Hand Path or Left Hand Path; Star Wars, Excalibur & Lord of the Rings

This essay was written around March 2001 when the Taliban destroyed the Buddhas of Bamyan in Afghanistan, (before 9/11 events). The actions of Taliban fitted with a myth cycle and conflict with Taliban was expected. A decade later this war continues. This essay is somewhat dated and my own views of LHP and RHP have developed and moved on. However, the essay is included here as it does represent some of the views and thinking that were prevalent in the pagan/magical scene of late 1990's and at turn of the century.

"O light of life: Be thou a bright flame before us: Be thou a guiding star above us: Be thou a smooth path beneath us; Kindle thou in our hearts within, A flame of love for our neighbour, To our foes, to our friends, to our kindred all: To all men on this broad Earth." Wiccan Book of Shadows

The other day, someone asked me 'what is the difference between the Left Hand Path and the Right Hand Path and exactly what is a White Witch?'

Perhaps the answer lies in the greater scheme of things, of what is right hand path and the left hand path. In pub moots and other pagan gatherings, we all ask each other *'what are your interests?'* Over the years I've heard all sorts of replies, from 'I am a Black Brother of Left Hand Path' to a 'White Witch and White-lighter'.

The image someone tries to portray is not a real state of affairs, and I for one don't take much notice of such descriptions in forming of my opinion of someone. A teenage boy who dresses in black and spends most of his time playing Dungeon and Dragons is not really a Black Brother (BB) of left hand path (LHP) in the way he thinks he is, or the white witch stock market-broker whose decisions could result in hundreds of third world farmers losing their livelihood is not exactly very white in the way he thinks he is. So if they are not left hand path (LHP) or right hand path (RHP) in the way they think they are, in what way are they LHP and RHP?

The far right or extreme form of the RHP or the White Brotherhood is about restriction, control and conditioning. The RHP brotherhoods like Klux Ku Clan, Islamic Taliban, and other obvious sects all have the same mentality, and, wearing white is not all they have in common. The extreme form of the RHP is based on one 'true way' and no compromise. So, what about LHP practitioners? This is a confusing term, as it originally derives from LHP Tantra, in which the goal of the magician is to break away from the social conditioning of Hinduism. Social conditioning is different for each person and culture; for example, some Hindu Tantrics eat fish as part of their practices. However, for a Western Tantric to eat fish would not be a taboo-breaking act, but, being a vegetarian can be seen as LHP act, as it breaks away from meat oriented western food culture where animals are reared in poor factory like conditions,; hence many pagans are vegetarians. Another example could be for a magician from an Islamic or Jewish background eating a 'bacon sandwich', I guess in some people's books that would make them a black magician!

As for the term Black Brother, the magician having crossed the Abyss might become attached to what lies here, and end up like the White Brothers. No one can start with the goal of becoming a black brother, if the magical intent is not pure the seeker is not even going get a foot out of the fortress of ignorance. Examples of Black Brothers are best seen in characters such as Darth Vader from *Star Wars* and Saruman the White of *Lord of the Rings*; both of whom had to journey long, and, had cross the abyss with pure intent. However it is after becoming a 'Jedi warrior' and crossing the abyss that a Black Brother might be formed, getting to the abyss itself can take lifetimes, let alone crossing it. The likelihood of running into a real Black Brother in the next pub moot is about the same odds as running to the Pope in s similar situation.

    I find all these RHP/LHP definitions rather tedious; I like the term 'grey path' myself, which expresses more of a balance between the energies. A RHP person told me once that the grey path is also LHP, as it is still sitting on the fence. From a RHP view, anything that will not conform into their one 'true model' of universe is not accepted. A LHP strand of the grey path would that the

159

practitioners still need to break way from more conditioning and control of RHP.

What is all this to do with paganism you may ask? Well I think the pagan movement since its beginning has been a very Grey path and some times LHP (in the Tantric sense not the Kabalistic sense). All of the founding fathers of the movement were not accepted socially by the establishment or white brotherhood, and were shunned by the patriarchal hierarchy of society. To name a few: Aleister Crowley (1875-1947) who was a bisexual libertine, Ross Nichols (1902 – 1975) who was a naturist; Gerald Brosseau Gardner (1884-1964) who was a naturist and interested in S&M, and Alex Sanders (1926-1988) who was bisexual; to feminist witches, and the highly -politically active witches like Star Hawk, all have their personality integrated into their magic. All have broken away in their own way from the socially acceptable patriarchal view.

Why is it now that pagans accuse each other of 'black magic'? As paganism spreads daily and it becomes more popular is it in-effect becoming more politically correct to be more acceptable and it is selling out! Whole orders shun use of magical plants (drugs), and alcohol is not acceptable in some pagan rites, were even the 'Great Rite in token' is replaced by some poor drumming.

By this rate, neo-paganism is going to end up like what its founders tried to get away from, merely replace the 'word' our Father in heaven with Mother in heaven! The shell might be changed, but we still have, the same patriarchal RHP mentality we started with.

Many pagans are fond of Merlin and Arthur and are happy to take on such magical personas; however, I for one, feel more akin to Mordred and Morgan Le Fey. There are many stories and myths connected to these characters and many interpretations are possible. For Example, we can examine the Arthurian myth cycle, one adaptation of the story *Le Morte d'Arthur* seen by many is the film *'Excalibur'*. Merlin, a figure who so many pagans aspires, to become, is portrayed as the typical 'all wise magician'. However, he uses the Dragon's breath/energy of the land to transform Uther Pendragon into the form of Gorlois Duke of Cornwall, so that Uther could fulfil his lust for Ingrain the wife of the Duke. Uther, in his transformed shape sleeps with Igraine without her consent: rape in another word. This makes Merlin an accessory to rape! Merlin was out of line here by his action! Arthur, the magical child is born nine months later, during which time Merlin is recovering from his rite. Soon after the birth, Merlin comes to court to claim Arthur as part of his pact with Uther; Arthur is forcibly removed from Igraine's arms. What of Igraine's 'True Will'? It seems that men around her make her decisions for her, the King Uther tricks and rapes her with help of Merlin and then she loses her baby. In the film, Morgan Le Fey, aged eight, is present at the rape of her mother, and rightly blames Merlin for this, she, being gifted with second sight knows transformation is a trick.

Later, Karma is returned when Morgan Ley Fey uses Merlin's trick and uses the Dragon's breath (evoked by the charm of making) to transform herself into the form of Guinevere and sleeps with her half brother, Arthur, to conceive a son. Merlin receives his karmic return and gets frozen in ice by Morgan Le Fay. It seems that no one bats a eyelid when Arthur is conceived this way, but when karma is returned and Morgan Le Fay conceives the next King everyone is up in arms. Alpha men don't like women in control and the Grail quest begins to save the land. The 'white knights' die, one by one, in the quest for the Grail, the search for the Goddess of the Land, even though Morgan Le Fay is the Goddess of the Land at this stage. This is not acceptable to the White Knights and Arthur, and the Grail (Goddess) has to be found and controlled, placed in a box on a Christian altar in Camelot. The Isis/Horus ruler ship of Morgan Le Fay and Mordred is seen as evil. Freud discussed the jealousy and fear of Fathers toward their Sons as well as the love of Mother/Son (Oedipus complex). The dominant father (patriarchal system) expects the sons to be like their father and the mothers not to interfere in the 'Manly' development of the sons. The patriarchal model is never tolerant, and would destroy anything that does not conform. Morgan Le Fay's followers are seen as 'Black Knights' that must be stopped. Merlin, if not frozen would probably come and take Mordred form Morgan Le Fay to ensure he would have become another Arthur.

Morgan Le Fay's son Mordred, like Arthur, is a 'moon child', and as son of Arthur indeed has the right to the throne. Meanwhile, the land is suffering, as the King is married to the land, but the King by now is impotent (loss of Excalibur) and the land can no longer be fertilised. Mordred comes to Camelot, the young sun/son (Horus) to claim his birthright, however Arthur (Osiris) refuses and breaks the myth cycle (as Arthur is completely Christian now), and decides to fight Modred. Now Mordred is portrayed as Seth rather than Horus and Morgan Ley Fay as Nephthys. The battle of the two armies leads to death of both father and son, and loss of the 'magical ruler of the land'. Chaos follows and Christian patriarchal dominance of the Land becomes complete. Excalibur is returned to the Lady of Lake, the deep sea of our collective unconscious; Excalibur will resurface again when we acknowledge Mordred and Morgan Le Fay and allow them have their time of spiritual kingship.

In *Star Wars,* father and son, Darth Vader and Luke Sky Walker fight on many occasions. When Darth Vader asks Luke to join him so 'as father and son to rule' together, of course Luke refuses this offer as it would break the myth cycle. Darth Vader doesn't kill him, but only injures him so the myth cycle can continue. They both are serving the Force, the Land in their own way. The Emperor is the 'real' black magician of the RHP mentality who is not prepared to accept any other way apart from his own, and, like all RHPs in fiction or real life is prepared to destroy the world to prove his point. This brings us back to the Taliban, and, other religious fanatics and all other RHPs who would rather destroy the world if it doesn't fit in with their own definition. The hero in *Star Wars* is Darth Vader who by sacrificing himself (Sacrificial King) and killing the Emperor, ensures that his son carries on the magical line, and, the Universe remains intact. In magic, dark and light are not opposite, and, they are intertwined in path of magician which is grey.

Another fictional hero, Gandalf the Grey further illustrates this path. While a great magician and bearer of one of the Rings, he still has the title of Grey. After his battle with Balrog and the fall into the abyss he dies. He is, like Christ, a resurrected 'god' and no longer a magician. This is a state of light where the physical body no longer exists, and he is not just wearing white robes and should not be confused with our 'White Witches' title. Anyone who uses the One Ring the symbol of ultimate patriarchal dominance is consumed by it.

Arthur was unable to overcome his ego and wanted to remain king, while Darth Vader saved the universe and continued the myth cycle, Gandalf as a resurrected god ensures Frodo destroys the Ring.

To fully overcome the ego we cease to exist in the physical world; Christ and Gandalf returned from the death of their ego briefly as resurrected gods. The Sufi martyr Hallaj at the moment of overcoming his ego, declared himself god. The physical world ceased to exist and was no longer was able to function, he was mad in eyes of the world and death by hanging for blasphemy soon followed. We struggle with our egos all the time, and we try to be aware of it. The next time after a successful ceremony when you think as a Arch this or Master Magus that you are beyond your ego, try walking on water, if you manage it then let the media know, otherwise stop kidding yourself, staying in Yesod 'realm of imagination' is fun but Kether is long way away.

If it's all crap, than why bother? Well, Daniel Son, dear grasshopper, when all your truths and illusions have been shattered perhaps then you can begin thy journey, now wax on, wax off..... so I keep digging until I hit something that my shovel doesn't go through. As it says in Terry Pratchett's *'small gods'* The Turtle Moves (De Chelonian Mobile).

LHP and RHP revisited

At the beginning of this essay, I mentioned my views on LHP and RHP, which have developed and moved on from their late 90's position (as outlined in the above material). Now I will discuss my current view (2010).

In my current view, the LHP v RHP position actually misses half the dynamic. There are number of political spectrum models around (e.g. Nolan chart, Political Compass, Pournelle chart), and these models can be applied to the RHP v LHP magical argument too. What I found most helpful was that whole range is presented in the political spectra models and the 'relative position' is given. Even if we separate the magical path and political view, these models are still useful.[119] There are four position/areas, not two!

---

[119] http://en.wikipedia.org/wiki/Political_spectrum and http://en.wikipedia.org/wiki/Nolan_Chart and http://www.politicalcompass.org/ and http://en.wikipedia.org/wiki/Political_compass

The Political Compass (http://www.politicalcompass.org/) model is rather useful in developing this thinking. Especially before reading on please look at the graph of international leaders in relation to each other on the political compass:

http://www.politicalcompass.org/images/internationalchart.gif

We can try to use political theory to look at RHP/LHP as there is an overlap between magic and politics. Observing elections is like watching the shifts in the collective subconscious. Millions of people focused on single act of voting for their parties of choice, their ideals. Making a cross on a parchment, creating a talisman called a ballot paper. Using oldest and simplest form of Sympathetic magic, a colour=an idea. Red, Blue, Yellow, Green, all just flying tribal flags. Now the counting, holding the breath as we stand on the edge, energy swirling. In many countries religion and politics are joined at the hip, for example Church and State, the Caliphate, and other religious bodies which run countries and pass laws.

Let us now apply the political compass principle to magic, as a magical compass. The key point in political spectra models are to shift the thinking from only left v right, which is from one axis to two axes (biaxial). So there is above (authority), and below (libertarian) as well as right and left thinking. To apply this approach[120] in a magical context:

---

[120] http://en.wikipedia.org/wiki/Political_compass

'Left' is defined as the view that the magical groups/covens/etc should be run by a cooperative collective or a network of communes/groups. For example, Pagan Federation, Council of British Druid Orders, where number of groups are working together.

'Right' is defined as the view that the magical groups/covens/etc should be left to the devices of individuals and organisations. For example, most magical orders, covens or groups which are focused on developing their own orders or groups and keep to themselves with little interaction with other groups.

The other axis (Authoritarian-Libertarian) measures one's magical opinions regarding a view of the appropriate amount of personal freedom: 'Libertarianism' is defined as the belief that personal freedom should be maximised (create your own magical system) and follow 'Do What Thou Wilt Shall be the Whole of Law, Love is the Law, Love Under Will'.

While 'Authoritarianism' is defined as the belief that authority and tradition should be obeyed (follow a set of Holy Books, or a Guru or a Prophet e.g. Jesus stating, the only way to the Father is through him).

I wonder if most people's concerns are mainly around the Y axis (Authoritarian v Libertarian) rather than the X-axis (one collective or several closely linked groups, versus independent separate groups). The point to bear in mind is the 'relative' positions. To make it easy for illustration, let's examine the above graph example[121] for Nelson Mandela and the Dalai Lama if person X fell right of Nelson Mandela but Left of the Dalai Lama, Nelson Mandela could say X is a brother of RHP, while the Dalai Lama could say X is a brother of LHP; even though all 3 are in the left/libertarian part!

Here is my own score on the political compass test: Economic Left/Right: -8.25. Social Libertarian/Authoritarian: -5.08 which is in the bottom left corner. That is left of both Nelson Mandela and Dalai Lama, which would be make me LHP as far as they are concerned. A person with a score of -7 is right of me and from my perspective, they are RHP, while someone with score of -9 falls on the left of me and from my perspective, they are LHP; even though we are in the left/libertarian part of the graph or path. It's all about understanding the 'relative' positions, which allows us to relate to other people views and understand where they are coming from. It's worth taking the test, it is interesting.

With regard to specific groups, traditions, etc, in my view, the RHP power/strength is based on collective strength, while the LHP power/strength is based on individual power. To use a Sci-fi reference, this explains why the Jedi are a huge group (whole schools) while the Sith work as pairs of two (apprentice and master).

---

[121] http://www.politicalcompass.org/images/internationalchart.gif

Both the RHP and the LHP of course have their pros and cons. There are pitfalls in both the RHP and the LHP. The challenge is to avoid the pitfalls of whatever path one follows.

To Genes, Memes, Gods and beyond (Sex, Chocolate & Religion)

This essay was written in 1999.

'I was a hidden treasure, and I wanted to be known'-Sufi proverb regarding world creation.

This essay tries to look for a rationale for spirituality. Perhaps the aim of 'a seeker after truth' is one that achieves greater understanding, an understanding that has its roots in experience and knowledge rather than blind faith. This is beautifully seen in the Sufi proverb: 'One who knows thyself knows thy Lord'. The search for any form of truth be it scientific, philosophical or religious is one that has shaped human life in its multitude of diversity.

The centre of scientific truth is the doctrine of validation: the ability to reproduce an observation and test a hypothesis. A reproducible finding consists of a 'truth'; addition of solution A to B always gives C under stated conditions. This simple approach has been so successful that it has resulted in increased levels of our perception of our reality, from atoms, to images of the earth from the moon and beyond. In case of null hypothesis, a 'truth' is only found when the experimenter rejects it.

The philosophical truth's focus is less defined, in its most reductionist form perhaps I=thought. While the position of religious truths are hugely varied, and depend on the approach taken. Here, it becomes clear that science, with its precise and methodical approach, has failed in its attempts to 'enlighten' the world. The products of science affect our lives every day, yet very little effects our 'self'. The worlds' atheist population is minute, and certainly not increasing rapidly enough to match the speed at which religions spread. The truth offered by religions is one that the vast majority of humanity has accepted.

Some mystics say: 'The only Truth is that there is no Truth.' The learning process might be speeded up, not by seeking the truth, but by thinking that everything is a lie or illusion.

Maybe, for one moment we should suspend disbelief, and look for the Gods. A fascinating 'protocol' for searching for god is described in A.Crowley's book *'Magick in Theory and Practice'*, in the operation of *Liber Astarte*. Here, the philosophus is asked to think of a deity, any god or anything that represents a higher being to them, and the process of choice is random, it could be a deity from any period in history or culture. For example, a deity from the Hindu pantheon, or an ancient Egyptian god, the Greeks, Celtics, Romans, Christ, Allah or Jehovah. The *Liber Astarte* is about the practice of devotion to the deity of choice, building a relationship with it, and eventually having 'faith' in and reaching unity with it. There is a time limit of one year on this practice, after which the philosophus is supposed to abandon the operation and look back at the process and experiences. There are seven stages in the relationship:

'First, an Imprecation, as of a slave unto his Lord.

Second, an Oath, as of a vassal to his Liege.

Third, a Memorial, as of a child to his Parent.

Fourth, an Orison, as of a Priest unto his God.

Fifth, a Colloquy, as of a Brother with his Brother.

Sixth, a Conjuration, as to a Friend with his Friend.

Seventh, a Madrigal, as of a Lover to his Mistress.

And mark well that the first should be of awe, the second of fealty, the third of dependence, the fourth of adoration, the fifth of confidence, the sixth of comradeship, the seventh of passion."[122]

Anyone can carry out this practice and most that have carried it out have reported experiences of the 'divine', vivid dreams with the deity of choice, 'miracles', and many other strange synchronicities. The students of Chaos magic have had success with even fictional deities such as Cthulhu created by writer H.P. Lovecraft, or using archetypes based on the characters from *Star Trek,* hence, demonstrating the 'process' of belief is as important as the 'subject' of belief itself.

The development of the relationship with a deity is said to follow seven steps: first is one awe, second of fealty, third of dependence, forth of adoration, fifth of confidence, sixth of comradeship, and seventh of passion; so it appears that within a space of one year anyone can from a relationship with a any deity and have a deep spiritual experience. In the spirit of experimentation, I carried out

---

[122] Crowley, Aleister, Magick in Theory and Practice, Red Wheel/Weiser, 1994, p617.

the *Liber Astrate* operation for one year, the deity I chose (or perhaps the deity who chose me!) was/is Mithras, a Persian Solar god of Truth, Love and Light.

Maybe Gods work not only because they can 'act as opium of the masses', but as they are key in our deep collective subconscious. By opening ourselves to the divine, something incredible occurs, which has a deep psychological effect to say the least; maybe we have created god in our own image and not vice versa. Perhaps the 'divine' is like an ocean, and, when we try to drink from it, we become the drinking vessel acting as a cup, we give the divine its shape and colour. The Indians ask Alexander the Great which god he worshiped and he said 'Dionysis' and described him, the Indians replied: 'yes we know Shiva'. Humankind is able to make connection to the 'other' and look at the same divine ocean and see and experience different things, and then sometimes declare his/her particular deity as the sole god. (The cause of many holy wars and death.) In the heart of most religions lies a mystical branch, Gnostic Christians, Jewish Kabbalist, Sufi Muslims, Buddhists, and Pagan Magicians to name a few, all of which emphasis the individual's experience of the divine. Despite the differences in their approach, these mystics seem to get on well with which each other, unlike the orthodox members of the same religions. The mystics way is a hard one, from Mohammed's cave retreats, to Jesus wandering in the desert, to Buddha sitting under a tree. The road to self discovery and making connection to the divine is filled with pitfalls and difficulties, also as the Merlin says in the film *Excalibur*: 'the way of necromancer is a lonely one'. The difficulty, hardship, and its apparent lack of reward to those who are not in mysticism could explain why mysticism has always been on the fringes of organized religion and human culture. Prof. Richard Dawkins in *'The Selfish Gene'* states: 'Most of what is unusual about man can be summed up in one word: 'culture'.... Cultural transmission is analogous to genetic transmission (sex) in that, although basically conservative, it can give rise to a form of evolution.'[123] Working on the same theme Dr. Susan Blackmore hits the nail on the head in her book the *'Meme Machine'*.

Memes are described as an element of culture that may be considered to be passed from brain to brain by non-genetic means, that is by any means of copying, especially imitation. In mystical terms, memes could be said to represent attachments, things that distract from ones true Self, and create a world of 'I' and 'You'. A comical example from popular culture is the Homer Simpson character from the *'The Simpsons'* cartoon. Homer is heavily attached to chocolate cookies, at one point he tries to stop himself from eating them by electrifying the cookie jar. However, soon afterwards he wants them, so he tries to open the jar and gets electrocuted, but he tries again and gets electrocuted again, he keeps doing it again and again while repeating to himself his meme: 'cookies, cookies.'

---

[123] The Selfish Gene by Richard Dawkins, (OUP Oxford; edition, 1989) p189.

Complex religious ideas or religious memes have co-evolved with genes, which increase their number. Dr. S. Blackmore states:

'There are several ways in which memes might influence genes. Priests attain power and status by predicting (or appearing to predict) weather, disease, or crop failure; by building or being associated with temples and other grand buildings; by wearing expensive and impressive clothes; and by claiming supernatural powers. In many cultures the priests or rulers are given divine status. We know that woman prefer to mate with high-status men, and that these men leave more offspring, either by having more wives or by fathering children by women who are not their wives. Even in societies in which the priesthood is celibate and could not (or at least should not) pass on their genes, other people could acquire power by association. If this religious behaviour helped people acquire more mates, then any genes that inclined them to be more religious in the first place would flourish. In this way genes for religious behaves would increase because of religious memes.'[124]

If there is a really 'religious genes' in some people, genes that have given their bearer some survival advantage during times of crisis. Then perhaps instead of fighting the instinct to believe, and use logic to hammer the 'need to believe' as Richard Dawkins and others do, perhaps the stratagem to overcome religious dogma should be belief in a deity of choice e.g. goddess of chocolate, and the religious dog inside a fictional bone!

---

[124] The Meme Machine by Susan J. Blackmore Oxford University Press (1 May 1999), p197.

Religions encourage large families, and encourage the notion that those who are not of the same faith are evil non-believers who need to be converted or killed! Jesus's comment about 'the only way to the father being through him' is emphasized more than his view about turning the other cheek or loving thy neighbours. The religious fundamentalists have heaven waiting for them, so they would fight bravely, and usually win against those who are more concerned with their self-interest or the liberal mystics. The mystics, no matter what their religious background will always remain a small group of people who are mostly seen as heretics and are persecuted. One has to ask oneself, is it worth the hassle to leave the Orthodox religion, our social conditioning and embark on the Gnostic journey? (Ignorance is bliss after all!) Once one leaves the fortress of ignorance behind on the path toward the forest of enlightenment there is no turning back, as beautifully illustrated by character Cypher and his desire to return to his illusions in the film 'The Matrix'.

Once invoked, Ganesh, the elephant headed Hindu god rushes through the forest and destroys all illusions as he moves. All decent spiritual teachers warn the student about the pitfall, and rightly try to discourage them from setting out on the journey. My experience was no exception, when I met my first formal potential spiritual teacher. Martha said:

'At your age you should be going to night clubs and partying, rather than joining our healing and psychic development group. You should have fun while you are young and when you get to our age then you should join a spiritual development group.'

I almost fell off my chair at Martha's suggestion, it had taken me weeks to find her and get an appointment. She was one of the most popular spiritual healers and mediums in London. I had to run all the way from school to get to the appointment on time and still had my school uniform on and I, a seeker of 'truth' was hoping for some teaching from her lessons in divination and healing. She was a pleasant looking lady in her sixties, of large stature and with her blue dress and pearl necklace she fitted the stereotype of a medium very well. Her suggestion to me, partying, was not what I had expected. Sadly I ignored her advice, and didn't follow the path of the 'teenager' she suggested. Well if I had followed her advice you wouldn't be reading this right now! And I would have had spent even more time getting drunk and being a tart! (Which might have better after all, maybe I should have listened to her).

I left her house determined to find another teacher; I could see Martha's point, the average age in her group was fifty and I was fifteen. Eventually, Martha realized I wasn't going to give up, so she gave me number of another medium, who did have younger members in her group, well, members in their thirties. 'Seek and you shall find' I said to myself, as I made my way across London. Jane did take me under her wing, a medium and healer at night and a social worker by day; she wasn't bothered by my age.

So, we started out on mediations and working while listening to the following guided visualization: 'Close your eyes and imagine you are walking down a country lane, its spring, and you are walking into a walled garden....' (Green Sleeves was playing on the stereo.)' So with that, my magical journey started.

The mystical journey is perhaps the greatest adventure anyone can take part in; the voyage of self-discovery. As C.S. Lewis said in *'Til We Have Faces'*: 'How can the gods meet us face to face till we have faces?' Once we have our face, then we can have a relationship with the divine, on a stable footing, without the use of fear of hell or the desire for heaven; to love god for love's sake, not because of what he will do or not do for us. There is still the need to be wary of the pitfalls of such interaction; one person's god is usually another's demon! This note of caution is most amusingly seen in several of Terry Pratchett's books such as *'Small Gods'* or for example his Granny Weather Wax character saying of: 'you don't want to go around believing in gods, it only encourages them.' The relationship between the divine and us is one of self-examination, while the divine is at the same time is reaching for us. As the Sufis say 'for every step you take towards god, god takes a hundred steps towards you.' As to what happens when people forget god, the following passage form R.Kipling's *'Puck of Pook's Hill'* is example of one possible humorous outcome:

' "Smith of the Gods," I said (Puck), "the time comes when I shall meet you plying your trade for hire by the wayside."'

'What did Weland say?' said Una. 'Was he angry?'

'He called me names and rolled his eyes, and I went away to wake up the people inland. But the pirates conquered the country, and for centuries Weland was a most important God. He had temples everywhere - from Lincolnshire to the Isle of Wight, as he said and his sacrifices were simply scandalous. To do him justice, he preferred horses to men; but men or horses; I knew that presently he'd have to come down in the world - like the other Old Things. I gave him lots of time - I gave him about a thousand years - and at the end of 'em I went into one of his temples near Andover to see how he prospered. There was his altar, and there was his image, and there were his priests, and there were the congregation, and everybody seemed quite happy, except Weland and the priests. In the old days the congregation were unhappy until the priests had chosen their sacrifices; and so would you have been. When the service began a priest rushed out, dragged a man up to the altar, pretended to hit him on the head with a little gilt axe, and the man fell down and pretended to die. Then everybody shouted: "A sacrifice to Weland! A sacrifice to Weland!'

'And the man wasn't really dead?' said Una.

'Not a bit. All as much pretence as a dolls' tea-party. Then they brought out a splendid white horse, and the priest cut some hair from its mane and tail and burned it on the altar, shouting, "A sacrifice!" That counted the same as if a man and a horse had been killed. I saw poor Weland's face through the smoke, and I couldn't help laughing. He looked so disgusted and so hungry, and all he had to satisfy himself was a horrid smell of burning hair. Just a dolls' tea-party!

'I judged it better not to say anything then (that wouldn't have been fair), and the next time I came to Andover, a few hundred years later, Weland and his temple were gone, and there was a Christian bishop in a church there. None of the People of the Hills could tell me anything about him, and I supposed that he had left England.' Puck turned, lay on his other elbow, and thought for a long time.'[125]

Perhaps Neitzche was right and 'we can kill god'. But, in doing so we perhaps kill part of ourselves? Can we liberate ourselves from the memes of orthodox religions or our social conditioning without cutting our own heart out? S.Blackmore like Buddhists, Sufis or many other schools of mysticism suggests simple meditative techniques based on observing and examining of the 'self' to release one's attention from one's false self. She states: 'learning to pay attention to everything equally stops self-related memes from grabbing attention; learning to be fully in the present moment stops speculation about the past and future of the mythical 'I'. These are tricks that help a human (body, brain, memes) to drop the false ideas of 'selfplex,' the quality of consciousness then changes to become open, and spacious, and free of self. The effect

---

[125] Puck of Pook's Hill by Rudyard Kipling, (1906, Kessinger Publishing Co, 2004), p17-18.

is like waking up from a state of confusion- or waking from the meme dream[126]....one of the effects of this way of leaving is that you stop inflicting your own desires on the world around you and the people you meet. This alone can mean quite a transformation'[127]. It is by being free of one's ego, desires, and attachments, that one can become in-tune with one's true Will. Perhaps the nearest thing to a truth or law is to do as one's true Will, while every other action is adding more bars to one's golden cage. If it's all about losing the self, what of god? Maybe when there is Silence inside one, and all attachments and fears are gone, there is a place where the Divine is said to be present, sitting right in front of you, staring back at you. What you call 'god' has always been with you since the beginning, it is your self made perfect, there is no I or You, the rain drop reaches the ocean and becomes one with it. Or, as S. Blackmore puts it: 'we can be truly free -not because we can rebel against the tyranny of the selfish replicators (memes/genes) but because we know that there is no one to rebel.'[128]

    The same theme is followed by R. Dawkins in *'Unweaving the Rainbow'*, where he argues Keats was wrong in accusing Newton that reducing the rainbow to its prismatic colours lost all the poetry of rainbow. In fact science is and / should be the inspiration and basis of great poetry. To understand the mechanism of a process adds even more dimensions to it. There maybe no gold at bottom

---

[126] The Meme Machine by Susan J. Blackmore, (Oxford University Press, 1999), p243.
[127] The Meme Machine by Susan J. Blackmore, (Oxford University Press, 1999), p245.
[128] The Meme Machine by Susan J. Blackmore (Oxford University Press, 1999), p246.

of the rainbow now, but Newton's unweaving of the rainbow has been the inspiration and basis for much cosmology, and, even a bigger source of beauty; Ganesha, the destroyer of ignorance would have liked Newton! In science, as one-door closes, a hundred open, as soon as one question is answered, it leads to many further ones. For me the process of photosynthesis is one that holds great beauty, a great example of circle of life. Both in a physical and a mystical sense we are all star dust. I tried to write about the poetry of photosynthesis back in 1997 while, like Merlin, I was wandering madly in a forest. Merlin saw 'dryads' the tree spirits, while I faced with the same magnificence, I saw something even more amazing: Light and Life.

'Soul's Journey'

'I' a rain drop.

Fall down rapidly, the ground approaches,

the green grass so inviting,

falling on the soil, slowly sinking in,

Is this the end?

Tentacles reaching out in the dark,

one touches me.

I enter, the inevitable osmosis.

Travelling fast in the dark tunnel,

Then an upward rush, joining the xylem.

Surrounded by others like myself,

Up and up we go,

Walls giving off a faint green glow.

Becoming engulfed by green light the higher we go.

I see the end of the tunnel,

A bright light,

I slowly transform, becoming solid.

A food for others?

Photosynthesis.

This is called Soul's journey or through the Xylem (plant structures that allow water and minerals to travel from the root to leaves) and describes the events as a soul/rain drop comes down to earth from heaven (clouds) and changes through its journey, from the roots of a tree, joining other souls in the trunk of the tree and finally by photosynthesis in the leaf. Then, in presence of carbon dioxide changes into sugar (glucose) and releases oxygen. The light allows the raindrop to combine with the carbon and make glucose, the source of food for all life on earth. This is one of the poems from my poetry collection the *'Chocolate Scented Garden'*. Perhaps there are no tree dryads, or any gold at bottom of rainbows, but what we faced with is even more inspiring. In a poll, 40% of American Scientists who were questioned believed in a God that would answer payers; the truth only hurts when there is ego involved.

Prof. Dawkins finishes his *'Unweaving the Rainbow'* by saying 'Only human beings guide their behaviour by a knowledge of what happened before they were born and a preconception of what may happen after they are dead; thus only human find their way by a light that illuminates more than the patch of ground they stand on. The spotlight passes but, exhilaratingly, before doing so it gives us time to comprehend something of this place in which we fleetingly find ourselves and the reason that we do so. We are alone among animals in foreseeing our end. We are also alone in animals in being able to say before we die: yes, this is why it was worth coming to life in the first place.'[129] Perhaps this is what Sufis mean by saying: 'Die before you die'.

There are many fine examples that illustrate the heroes'/heroine's journey and the Gnostic Quest, from ancient myths, fairy tales, and folk stories to modern Hollywood movies. Joseph Campbell finds only one hero behind the thousand faces, the archetype of all human myths. It is by understanding this myth

---

[129] Unweaving the Rainbow: Science, Delusion and the Appetite for Wonder by Richard Dawkins, (Penguin Books Ltd, 1999), p153.

and making our own journey that we may find the key of the door of Holman's Hunt *'Light of the World'* which opens inwardly.

The story of the Gnostic quest is one we all hope to be part of, so the story is told again and again in all cultures and all periods of history. Perhaps it is the greatest memes of them all, the meme to replace all other memes! One of the most detailed stories of this quest is the Persian Faery tale: 'Simurgh'[130], or Joseph Campbell's 'Hero of Thousand faces', or Robert Bly's 'Tale of the Maiden King'.

---

[130] The Mysteries of Mithras: The Pagan Belief That Shaped the Christian World by Payam Nabarz, (Inner Traditions, 2005), pp71-85.

Spirit of Peace

My heart accepts all forms and faces;

My heart is a pasture for wild gazelles,

a monastery for Christian monks,

a temple for Pagan gods,

the Kabba for Muslim pilgrims

Tablets for the Jewish Law,

and pages for the Quran.

I proclaim the religion of Love,

and wherever it carries me,

this is my creed and faith'.[131]

  -by Ibn Arabi, (Sufi poet: 1165-1240).

'*This is our last best hope for peace'*

       - Babylon 5

This essay was written during 2000-2004.

---

[131] Translator unknown. Every effort has been made to trace holders of copyrights. Any inadvertent omissions of acknowledgement or permission can be rectified in future editions.

The first 'Spirit of Peace' conference took place at the Autumn Equinox 2000 with the theme of 'Light, Life, Love and Liberty'. The second conference took place at Samhain 2001, with the theme of 'Sacred Music & Art. The third conference took place at Autumn Equinox 2003, with the theme of the 'Nameless Path' and intent of marking United Nations Global Cease-Fire Day. The fourth conference took place at the Autumn Equinox 2004 to mark the United Nations Global Cease-Fire Day with the theme of 'The interface between Mysticism Religion and Magic'.

Spirit of Peace is devoted to the study of mysticism in all its aspects; literature, history, philosophy and practice; irrespective of religious denomination, label or name. Spirit of Peace is a non-profit making organisation, which was founded as a turn of the century project to create a space for the contemplation of inner and outer peace. We explore the rich tapestry of our diverse traditions, and the spirituality behind our beliefs. There can be no lasting outer peace without inner peace. To achieve world peace, each person needs to find their personal peace first.

We chose Amnesty International as the beneficiary of 2001 conference, and United Nations 'Adopt a Minefield' as the beneficiary of 2003 and 2004 events. These one-day annual charity events consisted of talks and workshops on mystical and esoteric traditions from around the world, bringing together mystics and esoteric practitioners from a variety of spiritual backgrounds. This provided a space where Christian Gnostics, Muslim Sufis, Jewish Kabbalists, Zen Buddhists, Hindu Shivaites & Tantrics, Pagans,

Druids, Shamans and all others who walk between the worlds could meet as one body. We aimed to create a space where ideas could be shared and inspirations may occur and bring us insights into ways of making this, a single blue tear in space we call 'our planet' a more peaceful place.

The Sprit of Peace web site:

http://groups.yahoo.com/group/spiritofpeace2k/

Spirit of Peace - background and history

'to seek, to know, to understand, to keep silent' – Aleister Crowley.

I have had the privilege of studying and sitting with a number of people over the years who walk the walk of a spiritual way of life. One learns wisdom from fools and stupidity from the learned! What does it really means 'to seek, to know, to understand, to keep silent'? Should we remain hidden, with our spark of light never to be seen? Should we stand in middle of a circle and read out a poem we have written as a bard? Should one tell the tale? Or would that be the ego speaking?

All journeys start with a desire **'to seek'**, and, if you are reading or working with esoteric material, you've probably done that already! You are on the path of 'change', knowing there must be more to life than whatever your experience of it was before. So, you sought and began to step out of your social conditioning, the norm. This is the unseen path that only you can thread. But beware;

don't spend all your life 'wandering', all quests have an ending, which may lead to many more beginnings. Find what you seek or at least find what you don't.

'To know', is what follows; the first fruits of the journey that you place in your backpack. We all know much; and, some are full of useful knowledge, almost a walking library. Some can tell you the names of all the religious pantheons, every occult book reference given, formulas of forgotten arts. Knowledge is the axe that you may take to break door of the house of ignorance. But beware not to become a stamp collector, filling your head with knowledge, and thousands or millions of books. When is it enough? How much can you place in your backpack before its sheer weight stops you from walking any further? What's the difference between a library and a person?

'To understand' seeking is to 'feel' the meaning, for the inspiration to grab you by the metaphorical balls, to feel fire in your heart, being aware of every hair on your body; your dreams are reality, a tango of sunlight and moonshine. Stars are falling all around you, and yourself are a shooting star, across the sky of time, and the moment of eternity.

'To keep silent', Many enlightened people have been killed for being 'heretics', while on a smaller scale anyone who sticks their head above the parapet gets egg on their face; therefore, it is no surprise that secrecy has always had a strong element in mysticism. It's much easier to remain in the secret garden, enjoying its fruits and the scents of its flowers, without the hassle of putting yourself in the firing line of other people's anger, criticism or endless other things that can be projected upon anyone who chooses not to keep silent. But then something moves you, and the words of your teachers ring in your ears, 'Service, Service' there is nothing more important than act of service to all creatures great or small on the earth, or one's fellow humans, the Great Spirit or one's god. So, wear your metaphorical flak jacket and step outside.

Many moons ago a Druid teacher of mine said: 'you have been spending lots of time in the cauldron being cooked, it's about time you brought something out of it.' When I asked what sort of thing she meant, she replied: 'most people at this stage bring out a gift for the community, a poem, song, story or something more universal like healing, or planting trees. It's up to you, go and meditate, come back when you know what inspiration from the cauldron you would like to make manifest in the world.'

Several weeks passed, one afternoon sitting at the centre of my circle all I could hear was the sound of the sheep, a fly zooming around, the occasional call of a crow, and the gentle twitter of a sparrow. Ancient oak and ash, many varieties of pine, hawthorn, apple and sycamore populated the green hills I faced, clouds gently floated by across the heavens, all was at peace. The angry young man, the rebel without a cause, a destroyer of patriarchy, the heavy metal head-banger, seems rather happy just sitting there! No strange drugs, no loud night-club music, no scantily clad bodies, no brightly lit computer games or mindlessly violent Hollywood movies, no shouts of football triumphs, no dying screams or battle cries of the million war 'martyrs', no shouts of hatred of others, no blaming of others, no double espressos to keep the eyes open, no shares in the petroleum industry, or clothes from sweat shops! Finally no guilt for still being alive! I let go of my anger towards those who destroy and exploit life, for those who kill in name of religion or god, letting it all go, and then listening to the silence......Allowing the inner peace to come through ...... Just sitting and being, action in inaction: the effortless effort, being in the moment.

My gift from the cauldron was help to manifest inner peace and outer peace; the spirit of peace that has always existed. To make this manifest in the physical world I organised the first mystics Sprit of Peace conference, an esoteric multi-faith gathering of mystics from different traditions.

I am walking my talk; but does organising such events does really make the world more peaceful? Does it make a difference to the sectarian violence in Northern Ireland? Or the Palestinian/Israeli conflict? Are there fewer muggings and fewer fights in our streets? Who knows, maybe not! The important thing is that I have broken out of 'my' circle of violence and ego! I am now part of the solution and not part of the problem; this change in outlook is about all anyone can do on an individual level. One can be shown where the door is, but in the end it's up to each individual to decide whether to walk through it, we do have free will after all! Tomorrow there will still be thousands of people killed by the action or inaction of other humans. We all carry a light inside ourselves, we could let the light out, and at the same time let go of our egotistical attachments, such as our anger; otherwise our ego and memes will rule us. As the Tantrics say, 'don't worry about changing the world; first make sure the world doesn't change you.' Both our inner and outer worlds are as we choose them to be to a great extent; we create our own reality. All our actions count, every wing beat of a butterfly has an effect, every drop of rain adds up in creating the larger intent of peace.

A Sufi teacher of mine once said that some of the so called religious leaders are like spiders, they try to catch people and feed on them, and eventually they create conflict. However, the Divine Being doesn't want us to hurt each other or any other creatures, as everyone and everything is part of the divine. The Divine Being doesn't cut off its nose to spite its face! So nor should we. Ya Hu.

Reviews of Spirit of Peace conferences.

The first, third and fourth Spirit of Peace conference were deliberately arranged to be near 21st of September, an auspicious time as this marks the time of Autumn Equinox. The time of balance and equilibrium; day and night, light and darkness are again the same length. This festival is called *Mehregan* (festival of Mithra) by Persians, while Celts and Druids called it *Alban Elued*, which means 'Light of Water'. It is also at this time that the initiates of the Eleusinian mysteries in Greece were shown an ear of grain and were told: 'In silence is the seed of wisdom gained.'

Spirit of Peace conference I: 'Light, Life, Love, Liberty'

The first Spirit of Peace event was held on 16th September 2000 at the Friends Meeting House in Oxford. This was a multi-esoteric conference focusing on the many paths to inner, outer peace and world peace, based on the esoteric/mystical aspect of each religion or philosophy. There were two concurrent sessions, and, at the end of the day there was a coming together. Many people contributed by reading a prayer, a poem, or an invocation from their tradition for inner peace and world peace. The final was everyone joining in a Dance of Universal Peace.

Our two concurrent sessions consisted of lectures and workshops First lecture was titled the 'Kingdom of heaven and Peace: Eastern Concept of Heaven, Hell and Royal Kingdom of God' by Ch. Rajinder Nijjhar, M.Sc. of Oxford Gnostic Association. Gnostics are the living Christ (satgurus) of Living God. For articles on sister Gnostic Christian and Sikh communities visit:
- http://www.nijjhar.freeserve.co.uk/gnostic.htm
http://www.nijjhar.freeserve.co.uk/sikhism.htm

Much discussion on the Gospel St. Thomas took place, indeed the Hollywood block buster 'Stigmata' draws much upon the Gospel of St Thomas and his teaching that Kingdom of God is within you and Kingdom of heaven is the world around you.

The Gnostic trend was followed by the next speaker, Terry Graham who gave a talk on 'Sufism'. Rooted in Islam, Sufism is a way to God through love. What can be considered, to some extent, a general definition of Sufis is: Sufism is a path towards the Truth where the provisions are Love. Its method is to look solely in one direction, and its objective is God. The Sufi is one who moves towards the Truth by means of Love and devotion. Since only one who is perfect is capable of realizing the Truth, the Sufi strives his utmost for Perfection. Terry Graham is a writer and filmmaker, and also a graduate of Harvard University in History and Literature. He has completed post graduate work in Persian Literature and written numerous articles on Sufism. He has translated 15 Sufi books from the original Persian into English. For further information see: http://www.Nimatullahi.org/

Next, Steve Wilson from the Fellowship of Isis gave an energetic and focused talk 'Peace from Chaos - how to get the peace we want from the Chaos we have'. Steve Wilson is one of the council of 32 Archpriest (ess) Hierophants who run one of the largest organizations of Goddess-worshippers in the world. He has also served the Goddess community for over a decade in public forums such as TV and Radio, open meetings and conferences as well as writing for newspapers and magazines. For further information see: http://www.fellowshipofisis.com/

The last talk before lunch was on 'Peace' by Richard Thompson, Warden of the Oxford Quaker Centre. He is the former Head of the Grange School in Bradford, where he implemented a highly successful Islamic-Christian prayer in this school. He is author of the forthcoming book: *'17 ways to develop my inner Strength: a book of self-development for young people'*. Quaker faith springs from the experience that each one of us can have a direct relationship with the Divine. Quakers find that by meeting together for communal worship they are empowered to find peace and strength for work in the world. For further information see: http://www.quaker.org.uk/

A complementary Indian curry lunch was provided by a Buddhist and Pagan cooks collaboration! After lunch we heard about 'Prophesy and the Qabalah: From the First Temple to the present day' by Akashanath. A brief look at the different manifestations of the prophetic tradition down through the ages, finishing with the role of prophecy in modern (magickal) Qabalah which is rooted in Judaism. For further information see:

http://www.cix.co.uk/~garuda

This was followed by a talk on 'Wicca and Paganism: A Contemporary Vision Quest' by Dr Katy Jennison. Katy is a practicing Wiccan and member of the Pagan Federation, and coordinator of the Oxford Wicca and Witchcraft Study Group. In the 1980s she was active in the UK Peace Movement. As an academic, her range has included English literature, Biophysics and Computer-Mediated conferencing, all of which she sees as relevant to the contemporary spiritual quest. Paganism celebrates the sanctity of Nature recognizing the Divine in all things; the vast, unknowable spirit runs through the universe, both seen and unseen. Such belief in the sacredness of all things can be found worldwide.

Contemporary Pagans interpret many of the beliefs and values of our ancestors in forms adapted to suit modern life, combining folklore, myth and archaeological evidence to generate new spiritual paths. What is important is not necessarily the historical lineage or political attainability of such visions, but the direction in which such inspirations channel human energy, human potential and human creativity. For further information see: http://www.paganfed.org/

A talk on 'Peace' by Mrs Helen Gething of Theosophical Society followed. The word theosophy has been used in the Occident for about 2,000 years to indicate knowledge of divine things or knowledge derived from insight and experience as well as intellectual study. It comes from the Greek *theos* (god, divinity) and Sophia (wisdom), and means divine wisdom concerning life from a standpoint of the divine consciousness which informs the universe. While the modern the theosophical movement can be traced back to Blavatsky and her teachers, it is part of a spiritual movement which is perhaps as old as thinking humanity. Its philosophy is a contemporary presentation of a perennial wisdom underlying the world's religions, sciences, and philosophies. Theosophical concepts are not dogmas; only the ideas that have value need be accepted.

Meanwhile in the workshop room we had a workshop by Eckankar on 'How to Master Change in Your Life', facilitators were Alan Church and Maria Arzayus. 'Eckankar, the Religion of the Light and Sound of God provides ancient wisdom for today. Eckankar always has a Living Eck Master whose mission is to help people find their way back to God. He gives personal spiritual guidance through dream study, Soul Travel and the Spiritual Exercises of ECK. A key teaching of Eckankar is that each human being is an individual Soul, a divine spark of God that lives throughout eternity. Eckankar teaches that through many lifetimes in the physical world, each of us progresses to a full realization and manifestation of our innate godlike qualities, especially divine love.' For further information see: http://www.eckankar.org.uk

Next was a Druid workshop by Matt McCabe of the Order of Bards, Ovates and Druids. Druids believe in the interconnectedness and sacredness of all life. Their work consists in the application and living of a system of teaching which has evolved and developed over many generations. The Order has two main aims. The first is to help the individual develop their spiritual, intellectual, emotional, physical and artistic potential. The second is to work with the natural world, to cherish and protect it, and to cooperate with it in every way - both esoterically and exoterically. For further information see: http://www.druidry.org/

This was followed by a workshop by Rev Chris Deefholts who is an ordained interfaith minister, with the Universal Brotherhood Movement, and works for the upliftment of the community through service and spiritual education. Her professional background is extensive and includes teaching Yoga and Meditation, Crystal and Gem Therapy, working with Flower Remedies, and teaching Reiki and other major Light Body Systems drawn from Huna, Tibetan, pre-Daoist, Angelic, Stellar, Egyptian,

Kabalistic and Hindu systems Her workshop consisted of a talk on inner and outer peace, explaining a little about the power of thought and energy, and then give the attendees the opportunity to receive an initiation after which they could switch on a Shakti to instil and invoke peace when they or the outer environment is stressed out. For further information see:

http://www.users.globalnet.co.uk/~dcvi/

The day was ended with a Dance of Universal Peace workshop by Daren Messenger. The dances were developed by Samuel Lewis; a Zen Buddhist Rishi and Sufi Murshid (teacher) and were derived from Sufi practices of Zeker. They use mantras and phrases from the world's spiritual traditions combined with simple movement and dance. They offer a safe way to experience a heightened awareness and a bodily understanding of spiritual being. They enable people to be open to each other in a moving and often joyous way. Daren Messenger lives for the call. Consequently he has had many occupations; from a computer network engineer, to a road sweeper. As a musician and poet, he has always been interested in the power of music to experience the divine. Currently he earns his living as an Existential Psychotherapist in North Hertfordshire. His studies in continental philosophy inform his approach to the interpretive nature of the dances. 'From the beginning of time, sacred movement, song and story have brought people together - at times of seasonal ceremony and celebration, as part of everyday life and life passages, in daily renewal and meditation, the Dances of Universal Peace are part of this timeless tradition. The Dances of

Universal Peace offer a safe way to be open to other people, creating trust and healing on a deep level. Through this dancing we come to know more of our true selves, so bringing peace, joy and unity to ourselves and to others. For further information see: http://www.dancesofuniversalpeace.org.uk/

After the first Spirit of Peace conference there was a huge interest and I felt there was need for another one. The theme chosen for the second conference was sacred music and art; as music and art allows communication between people from around the world, via their hearts rather than their heads! This is an expression of spirituality through the media of music, reaching for inner and outer world peace. A whole committee carried out the organization of next year's conference ~ we had formed an organization!

Spirit of Peace conference II: 'A Day of Sacred Music and Art', in aid of Amnesty International

Building on last year's day of lecture, and workshops, this year we celebrated by hosting a day of sacred music, poetry and art at the Holywell music room in Oxford on 10th November 2001. The venue was specially chosen as it is the oldest purpose built music hall in Europe, and indeed England's first concert hall. It was built in 1742 and numerous musicians, including Handel have played there, the hall has a peaceful ambience which we wanted to link to.

Figure 23: Holywell Music Room

Figure 24: Ivy clad Holywell Music Room

We used the media of music, poetry and arts as ways to explore the rich tapestry of our diverse traditions, and the spirituality behind our beliefs. We had chosen Amnesty International as the beneficiary of this year's conference, and all profits was donated to them. To conclude the day there was a 'jamming session' were all the musicians performed together in an improvised finale involving all the performers and members of the audience who wished to participate, using musical instruments or their singing voices!

The event featured:

Oxford Gamelan Society: Javanese Santiswaran chanting (Islamic), For further information see: http://bate.nsms.ox.ac.uk/ogs1.html

Oxford Drum Troupe: drumming beats from around the world.

For further information see:
http://www.southoxford.org/activities/odt.html

Anne Lister: She sings her own songs, which have a Celtic theme, to acoustic guitar. For further information see:
http://www.annelister.com

Byrd Chorus & Guests: Christian Early music group and instruments.

Burying Edward: new music steeped in Scottish and English folklore.

Oxford City Bell ringers: Change ringing on hand bells (mathematically permuted changes as would be performed on full-size bells in English Church towers). For further information see:

Spectral Vs Starlit Fire: Psycho-tronic cosmic wave electronic music.

Sam Holmes and Dan Fear: Banbury's acoustic duo, signing both traditional English Folk songs and their own songs.

Payam Nabarz: Sufi poetry of Islamic mystics: readings from Rumi, and other Sufi poets.

Lynn Elson: Oxford Poet and Storyteller.

It was very pleasant and highly inspiring day for all; and we had a very positive feedback, hence plans for a third conference were hatched. This was of course a month after the terrorist attacks of September the 11th, and peace was last thing in the minds of some.

When reflecting on post 9/11 events and as war in Afghanistan was gearing up, I wrote the following on 14th Oct 2001. It was aimed at the Taliban and intended to compare with Guild of Assassins and Marco Polo's tale of his encounter with them; sadly, it had the feeling of déjà vu about it. The earlier crime of Taliban destroying the Bamyan Buddhas was a clear indication conflict to follow.

Gods' game of Chess?

Here comes another war, humans pawns in gods' game of chess?

Athena, Brigantia, Macha sharpening their spears,

the Valkyres flying next to F15s,

Poseidon pushing battleships into place.

Agni putting gunpowder on his fire,

Kali destroying one world order to create a new one.

Descendants of Alexander and Genghis Khan

are playing soldiers again,

Riding on fast horses,

With Kalashnikovs on their shoulders,

High and invincible on opium and hash,

the gild of Assassins and Hashashins alive again.

Jumping off castle ramparts to their own death, to shock.

Bringing fear and terror to the Silk Road traders.

They call on Jehovah, Christ or Allah,

But are deaf to their gods reply:

Allah the most compassionate and merciful;

Christ the turner of the other cheek.

Marduk is spreading Anthrax,

Baal is demanding a blood sacrifice.

Holy books becoming weapons again,

Each page soaked with the blood of the 'infidel'.

Who are the Volorns, who are the Shadows?

Why can't the gods either help us,

or just leave our planet to us?

Perhaps they already have, or they never played chess with us.

Maybe everything is the way it is, because we humans want it that way,

Is this Free Will?

Spirit of Peace conference III: 'The Nameless Path', in the aid of 'Adopt a Minefield' project

The 3rd Spirit of Peace conference was held on 20th September 2003 at the Freinds Meeting House in Oxford, the date being chosen to mark the United Nation Global Cease-Fire Day (for further information see: www.peaceoneday.org). This one-day event was held in the aid of the 'Land Mine Trust' and consisted of talks and workshops from 'mystical' and 'esoteric' traditions from around the world. All profits were donated to the 'Adopt a Minefield' project.

The speakers were:

John Matthews on 'The People Of Peace: Meetings with the Sidhe'.

Two years ago John Matthews began to receive communications from powerful inner beings who called themselves the Sidhe, the ancient Irish name for the fairy people of these islands. Over a period of six months he took down a book length set of texts which dealt with the history of the Sidhe and their relationship and dealings with humanity. Now for the first time he will be reading from these unpublished writings and discussing the implications of the message to us all from this ancient race. Long known as "The People of Peace" they have much advice to offered to us concerning our own future in an endangered world. John Matthews is best known for his work on the Arthurian Legends, Celtic Spirituality and world mythology. He is the author of 70 books, including Wizards, The Quest for the Green Man, and Healing the Wounded King. He has been the historical advisor to the Jerry Bruckheimer movie of King Arthur, filmed in Ireland. He is married to the writer Caitlin Matthews with whom he has collaborated on numerous books, and they live in Oxford. For further information on John & Caitlin and their works visit their website at www.hallowquest.org.uk

Latif Bolat on 'Sufism (Islamic mysticism) & Sufi practices of music, dance & rituals'.

Latif is a Turkish Singer, Composer and Scholar of Turkish Music and Folklore. He is a native of the Turkish Mediterranean town of Mersin. After receiving his degree in Folklore and Music at Gazi University in Ankara, Turkey, he taught traditional music throughout the country. He then went on to manage Ankara Halk Tiyatrosu, a musical theater company, which performed traditional musical plays. Mr. Bolat also received additional degrees in Turkish History and Middle East Religion and Politics from Ankara University and an MBA from San Francisco State University. Now residing in the USA, Mr. Bolat is one of the most distinguished Turkish musicians in this country. His concert and conference itinerary has taken him all across America, Canada, England, Australia, New Zealand, Bulgaria, Indonesia and Turkey. Specializing in the ancient Turkish Mystic devotional music genre, he accompanies his singing on the baglama (long-necked lute) and has been received with appreciation and enthusiasm throughout the world, as he provides a unique philosophy and approach to the performance of traditional music. The California Art Council rewarded Mr.Bolat with a grant for his contributions to the preservation of Turkish traditional music. 'The flute of interior time is played whether we hear it or not.' - Kabir For further information see: www.latifbolat.com

Emma Restall Orr on 'Druidry'.

Emma was the Head of The Druid Network, former Joint Chief of British Druid Order, and author of Spirits of the Sacred Grove, Druid Priestess, Druidry: Re-Kindling the Sacred Fire, Principles of Druidry, Tides of Dying, and Ritual: A Guide to Life, Love and Inspiration. The Druid Network, and its root the British Druid Order, teaches and practices Druidry as the ancient native spirituality of Europe, re-kindling its sacred fire for the 21st century. For further information see: http://druidnetwork.org

Steve Wilson on 'Living Gnosticism & the Mandaeans'.

Steve is an author, broadcaster, jornalist, Magician, Druid, Pagan, Isian, Thelemite, MC of Secret Chiefs (Talking Stick as was), Tarot and Rune reader and lecturer. His own books are Robin Hood, Spirit of the Forest (1992) and Chaos Ritual (1993). He is one of the 32 Archpriest Hierophants who run the Fellowship of Isis and a founder of both the IOU Chaos Magic group and the Lovecraftian WID. He has appeared on most major UK TV and Radio channels as well as writing for both The Guardian and The Independent. He frequently takes his lectures to Fan Conventions, Schools, and anyone else who will listen. He also acts as Regional Co-ordinator for the Pagan Federation in South East London. For further information see: http://www.sethur.f9.co.uk/

Dr. Karen Ralls on 'The Templars and the Grail'.

Karen is an Oxford-based ancient and medieval historian and Celtic scholar, is author of *The Templars and the Grail* (2003), *Music and the Celtic Otherworld* (2000), *The Quest for the Celtic Key* co- authored with I.Robertson, 2001) and *Indigenous Religious Musics* (2001). She was a Postdoctoral Fellow at the University of Edinburgh (1995-2001), and Founder-Director of the Ancient Quest Institute, an organisation dedicated to the interdisciplinary exploration of science and spirituality & the Celtic and western spiritual traditions and their roots in the ancient world; music, tours, and storytelling featured. For further information see:

http://www.ancientquest.com/

Colin Low on 'Emanation and Ascent in Hermetic Kabbalah'.

Colin studied physics at the University of Western Australia and astrophysics at the Institute of Astronomy in Cambridge, UK. His professional life has revolved around computers, with four years as a consultant, 9 years as a lecturer in Computer Science at the University of London, and 13 years as an industrial researcher with Hewlett Packard. He has authored several academic papers and is named as inventor on 27 patents. Kabbalah has been a life-long passion. He began to take an interest in 1968, and studied and practiced it informally in a number of small groups before meeting a teacher in 1978. He studied and worked with her until her death in the early 90s. Colin states:"My life has been oriented around understanding the nature of the world and existence. Physics provides me with the tools I need to comprehend the natural world.

Kabbalah provides me with the tools I need to understand the inner world of my own being. I find no tension between the two. Neither is a definitive account of the world ... both are processes continuously ongoing in our mutual attempts to comprehend it."
Colin set up one of the first WWW Kabbalah sites in 1995, and it continues to be one of the top- ranked sites in this area. He has written *'A Depth of Beginning'*, a book-length introduction to Kabbalah that has been accessed extensively online, and translated into several languages. For further information see: http://www.digital-brilliance.com/kab

The evening world music concert featured:

Seagreen Singers (Christian Choir) with peace prayer.

Emma Chapman: playing folk violin

Latif Bolat: music of the Turkish mystics.

Bruno Guastalla: French Accordion.

Finale with Oxford Drum Troupe.

Spirit of Peace conference IV: The interface between mysticism-Religion-Magic, in the aid of 'Adopt a Minefield' project

The 4th Spirit of Peace conference was on 18th September 2004 to mark The United Nations Global Cease-Fire Day. This one-day charity event consisted of talks and workshops form mystical and esoteric traditions from around the world. Spirit of Peace has remained devoted to the study of mysticism in all its aspects: literature, history, philosophy and practise-irrespective of religious denomination, label or `name.' This year's theme was *'The interface between mysticism-religion- magic'*. All profits were donated to `Adopt a Minefield' project.

The speakers were:
Jane Clark spoke on 'Following the Religion of Love: The tradition of Muhyiddin Ibn 'Arabi'.

Jane is an editor, writer and independent researcher who has been studying the work of the great 13th century mystic and teacher, Ibn 'Arabi, for more than 25 years. She has had a particular interest in the interface between science and mysticism, working on such publications as 'Beshara Magazine' and the 'Journal of Consciousness Studies'. She is a student of the Beshara School, has recently studied for a masters degree in Arabic Thought at Oxford University, and for the past four years has been doing research on the early manuscripts of the Akbarian tradition. For further information see: http://www.ibnarabisociety.org/

Caitlin Matthews spoke on 'Ancestral Healing'.
Caitlin is a respected initiators in the Celtic and Arthurian traditions, and has opened many doors to a reappreciation of ancestral and mythic heritage. Caitlín's books include Singing the Soul Back Home, Celtic Devotional, and Sophia, Goddess of

Wisdom. John and Caitlin Matthews are the joint authors of The Western Way, TheEncyclopaedia of Celtic Wisdom, and The Arthurian Tarot. For further information see: www.hallowquest.org.uk/

Shahin Bekhradnia spoke on 'Zoroastrianism'. Shahin is a spokesperson for World Zoroastrian Organization. Shahin Bekhradnia was born in London of traditional Iranian Zoroastrian parents. As a main part of her religious upbringing, issues concerning pollution of the air, land and water entered her consciousness at an early age, long before such matters had been taken up by the media and before environmental organisations came into being in Britain. After taking a degree in Modern Languages at Oxford, she worked in Iran and then travelled round the world before returning to found a sixth-form and language college in Oxford. Her fascination with history and her encounters with people of different faiths and cultures focused her interest on the processes of identity formation, out of which emerged a doctoral thesis in Anthropology at St Anthony's College, Oxford on Identity Change among Iranian Zoroastrians in the 20th Century, on which subject she has lectured and published regularly. Most recently her research has focused on the Pamir Mountain area in Tajikistan. In recent years interfaith activities have taken some of her time and she has been actively involved with environmental organisations and issues for many years, both at village and national level, having contested district council elections and a General Election as a Green Party candidate.

Matt Lee spoke on 'The Academic study of Magic'. Matt was speaking on behalf of Society for the Academic Study of Magic (SASM). For further information see: www.sasm.co.uk Matt was a member of the Editorial Board of the Journal for the Academic Study of Magic and editor of the chaos magic 'zine Razorsmile. He is a film maker and philosopher from Brighton, just completing his doctoral studies on the work of Gilles Deleuze and is the regional co-ordinator for the Pagan Federation in the Brighton area. His interest is in techniques of belief-shifting, liminal experience and the relation of transcendence in both mystical practice and philosophical theory. His research is exploring the history of mystical practice in philosophy and the contemporary parallels and connections between the practices. For further information see: http://homepage.ntlworld.com/matt.lee7/

Michael Bingas spoke on 'Gods & Goddesses of Peace in Greek Mysteries'. Michael is an expert on the Greek mythology. He was a facilitator of Secret Chiefs speaker meetings in London.

The Revd David Platt from CND spoke on "Christians in the Peace movement". Movement'.

Workshops were led by the following facilitators:

Lesley Harris "Finding the divine within". Lesley has been a Hierophant in the Fellowship of Isis since 1999 and has been interested in developing her own spirituality since the 1970s. Currently she has a day job, but would like to help develop people on their own spiritual paths.

Sarah Verney Caird 'Voice Workshop-Sounding the Inner Silence' Using simple vocal exercises and movement we each make a strong connection to our core self. From this place we can together create a live sound meditation on Inner Peace. The workshop was followed by a short performance by Sarah and Susan Nares of Soundwell Healing Music in which workshop members were invited to participate as appropriate. Sarah Verney Caird is a singer who has worked as a Music Therapist for over 30 years, teaching, supervising and running workshops. She is also a sound healer and body worker, with a private practice in Oxford. Together with Susan and Oliver Nares, Sarah has co-founded 'Soundwell Healing Music' to further enable empowerment for change through music, therapy and sound healing. They have released their first CD: 'Unfolding Journey', for further information see: www.soundwell.net

The evening World Music Concert was given by:
*Dr. Andy Letcher: French bagpipes. Andy is a Troubadour and Bard and of Jabberwocky band fame. He is a freelance Researcher of Religious Studies; well known for his papers on Pagan Road protests.

Skeleton Crew: European Medival Folk Music. A group of amateur musicians of various sizes, with a mixed bag of acoustic instruments. They perform medieval, renaissance and baroque music (so called early music) as well as traditional folk music from many cultures and anything else they feel like. They play for public and private occasions, and are based in Oxford (UK).

Senegal: Jali Fily Cissokho 'voice & Kora'

Oxford Drum Troupe: West African polyrthmic rhythms

The day was a great success, with the threads between the talks weaving a rich tapestry of interlinked ideas; the musical finale allowed for a wild and free expression of the celebratory energies of togetherness. Summing up the events led me to the words of Rumi:

Not Christian or Jew or
Muslim, not Hindu,
Buddhist, Sufi, or Zen.

Not any religion
or cultural system. I am
not from the east
or the west, not
out of the ocean or up
from the ground, not
natural or ethereal, not

composed of elements at all.

I do not exist,
am not an entity in this
world or the next,
did not descend from
Adam and Eve or any
origin story. My place is
the placeless, a trace
of the traceless.
Neither body or soul.

I belong to the beloved,
have seen the two
worlds as one and
that one
call to and know,
first, last, outer, inner,
only that breath breathing
human being.[132]   -Sufi mystic - Jelaluddin Rumi - 13th century

Acknowledgments

I would like to thank all our speakers, performers and workshop coordinators for the four conferences; without whose participation

---

[132] Translator unknown. Every effort has been made to trace holders of copyrights. Any inadvertent omissions of acknowledgement or permission can be rectified in future editions.

these events would not have been possible. We are very grateful to Quaker centre for the use of their space in the Friends Meeting House.

I would also like to thank all whose who helped in coming together of these events, special thanks to the SOP committee Glyn, Lesley, Ali, Mike, Ann. Asha and Simon C for the posters, and all our stewards and helpers, Steve, Bruce, Mic, Chrissie, Linda, Mogg, Lesley, Paul, Alex, Katy, Gavin, Astrid, Amanda, Rob and anyone else who has helped in any of the Spirit of Peace Events. Final thanks go to the source of all light whatever name we chose to call it.

Spirit of Peace web site:

http://groups.yahoo.com/group/spiritofpeace2k/

Epilogue: A blessing to peaceful demonstrators

This is a blessing for all those wish to peacefully demonstrate for freedom but face violence from their oppressors. This is to give non-violent direct action activists the spiritual support to reach their goal of freedom and justice whatever nation or country they are in; Gandhi showed that passive resistance can work. It was written at the Summer Solstice 2009.

I call on Verethragna, as the Boar, may he rage through the ranks of the foot soldiers of oppressive regimes, may their riot shields shatter, may their helmets and visors mist up, may their body armour fall, may their batons slip out of their hands. May they break rank, rout and disperse.

I call on the goddess Anahita, lady of the waters, may she give courage to the demonstrators, may she help them to continue the struggle for freedom, may she provide love and nourishment to those already arrested and heading into the pits of the oppressor's prison. May she bring light into the prison cells.

I call on Mithra, may the lord of truth to walk beside all who are fighting the Great Lie that are the Dictatorial regimes, may he support all the demonstrators, journalists and bloggers who are telling the truth and let their messages reach out to the wide world.

I call on the Sun at his height, may his light and warmth feed the fire and passion of the demonstrators.

I call on Atar, lord of fire, to once again burn the three headed beast that stole the Divine Glory, may the right of rulership be returned to the people, their voices heard and votes counted.

I call on Vayu, lord of wind, to blow away deceit, to interfere with the military police helicopters and stop them flying, to shorten the breath of the riot squads and stop them chasing protestors. May the oppressors be out of breath, and be tired.

I call on Tishtrya, the star Sirius, lord of rain, summer Solstice marks your time, Tir take thy form of a Young Man/Woman, and march beside the Old and the Youth of the nations, as they march toward the black clothed military police. Show them how you overcame the darkness before.

I call on Homa, may she heal the wounded, may she remove the demonstrators bullet wounds and baton bruises. May she fuse the demonstrators with ecstasy and joy and remove fear from their minds.

I fly to of Mount Davamand and I call the gods of my Ancestors: Verethragna, Anahita, Mithra, Atar, Vayu, Tishtrya, Homa liberate your land. Return to thy rightful place and land. Thy children in their darkest hour, beg of thee.

Come in their hour of need, and hold the line against the coming hordes, thy temples shall be rebuilt and past glory restored. You have not been forgotten.

All this I call at Summer Solstice, the height of sun's power.

Any political correctness melts with images of the military police, beating and killing protestors.

My creed of love and peace, takes a tea break.

I see my arms transform into hawk's wings, my head into a falcon, each breath takes me deeper, as avenging Horus emerges. Shaking with love and anger for oppressed nations. It's Father's day tomorrow, so I take the mantel of Horus, son risen to avenge all the fathers killed and imprisoned by oppressing governments, Osiris the slain father and risen god. Horus with his right eye the sun and left eye the moon.

I flap my wings in face of black shirt military mob and momentarily blind them, so their aim misses their target and the protestors; my croak a distraction to the black shirts.

Once again, I repeat my call to the goddess Anahita, lady of the waters, may she give courage to the demonstrators, may she help them to continue the struggle for freedom, may she provide love and nourishment to those already arrested and heading into the pits of the oppressor's prison. May she bring light into the prison cells.

Once again, I repeat my call to Mithra, may the lord of truth to walk beside all who are fighting the Great Lie that are the Dictatorial regimes, may he support all the demonstrators, journalists and bloggers who are telling the truth and let their messages reach out to the wide world.

May there be peace in the East, May there be peace in the West, May there be peace in the North, May there be peace in the South, May there be peace throughout the whole world.

'Say always the name of the Friend-slowly, slowly;

with this alchemy change the copper of the heart into gold-

slowly, slowly.

Drink from the wine of Unity in the tavern of Oneness

so that "I and you" will be taken from your mind- slowly, slowly.'

-Sufi poet Dr. Nurbakhsh

Ya Hu

Index

Aban, 23, 24, 38, 39

Achaemenian, 26, 27

Ahriman, 47, 48, 50, 52, 53, 57, 150

Ahura Mazda, 22, 43, 44, 47, 48, 50, 53, 55, 56, 58, 65, 68, 150

Anahita, 22, 25, 27, 35, 38

Angel, 24, 55, 61

Aradia, 86, 124, 130

Artaxerxes, 26, 27

Artemis, 109, 132

Arthur, 19, 161, 162, 164

Astarte, 109, 132, 171

Atar, 22, 45, 58, 218, 219

Aten, 43

Ayahuasca, 143, 147

Azi Dahâka, 57, 58

Babylon, 51, 63, 64, 186

Blackmore, 174, 175, 180, 181

Book of Shadows, 90, 108, 110, 111, 114, 116, 117, 118, 125, 128, 131, 132, 134, 139, 157

brotherhood, 77, 160

Brugsmansie, 143, 144

Caspian, 23, 38

Cauldron, 20

Celtic, 7, 14, 20, 32, 107, 201, 205, 208, 210

Cerridwen, 20

Charge, 18, 108, 109, 112, 132, 134, 135

chocolate, 174, 175

Christ, 164

Christianity, 43, 51, 60, 143

Craft, 3, 78, 88, 90, 95, 103, 104, 105, 108, 118, 140

Crowley, 86, 87, 88, 89, 91, 97, 98, 99, 100, 135, 136, 137, 138, 139, 160, 171, 188

Daevas, 41, 42, 49

Darth Vader, 159, 163

Datura, 143, 144, 145

Dawkins, 174, 175, 181, 184

Deeg Jush, 7, 8, 9, 21

Dervish, 15

Devas, 42, 151

Divine, 195

Doreen Valiente, 90

Dragons, 158, 161

Druid, 3, 10, 78, 92, 93, 94, 99, 138, 167, 190, 197, 207

Druids, 3, 8, 92, 94, 107, 139, 188, 192, 197

Dughdova, 43

ego, 164

Eid Didnay, 15

Equinox, 14

Faravahar, 61

Freemason Hall, 82, 87, 104, 118

Freemasonry, 1, 2, 77, 78, 79, 83, 85, 87, 88, 89, 91, 92, 93, 94, 99, 100, 101, 102, 104, 105, 106, 107, 108, 110, 111, 112,

222

113, 114, 116, 117, 118, 119, 131, 137, 139, 140

Gandalf, 164

Gandhi, 217

Ganesh, 176

Gerald Gardner, 88, 89, 90, 100, 105, 108, 110, 111, 114, 116, 117, 118, 125, 128, 131, 132, 134, 139

Glastonbury, 18, 19

Gnostic, 100, 102, 103, 135, 136, 139, 140, 173, 176, 184, 185, 193, 194

Goddess, 3, 18, 24, 26, 28, 34, 36, 37, 39, 70, 77, 109, 110, 131, 132, 133, 134, 135, 162, 194, 210

Golden Dawn, 3, 79, 82, 83, 84, 85, 88, 90, 94, 98, 104, 105, 106, 138

Great Rite, 160

Haji Firoz, 14

'Haji Firoz, 14, 22

Hale Bopp, 18

Hallaj, 164

Herakles, 70

Hermetic Order of the Golden Dawn, 79, 84

Hindu, 42, 158, 171, 176, 187, 198, 214

Hollywood, 193

Homa, 45, 55, 149, 150, 151, 152, 153, 154, 155, 218, 219

Horus, 18, 162, 163, 219

Hu, 12, 15, 19, 20, 22, 192, 221

initiate, 20

Isis, 3, 49, 51, 70, 84, 162, 194, 207, 213

Islam, 32, 35, 43, 51, 60, 194

Jesus, 20

Kabbalah, 16, 19, 208

Khider, 7, 22

left hand, 65, 100, 121, 126, 157, 158

Liber, 98, 136, 137, 139, 171, 173

Light, 21, 193, 196, 197

London, 16, 20, 25, 66, 67, 72, 79, 83, 85, 87, 88, 89, 92, 93, 177, 207, 208, 211, 212

Love, 10, 11, 12, 18, 120, 131, 133, 135, 167, 173, 186, 187, 193, 194, 207, 210

Luke Sky Walker, 163

Magic, 3, 88, 89, 102, 123, 124, 126, 139, 140, 147, 156, 187, 207, 209, 212

Marduk, 63, 64, 203

meditation, 198

Mehr, 38

Merlin, 161

milk, 24

Mithra, 8, 18, 27, 28, 30, 32, 38, 39, 41, 42, 45, 52, 60, 63, 64, 65, 66, 67, 68, 69, 71, 72, 73, 74, 75, 192, 217, 219, 220

Mithraeum, 74, 114

Mithras, 3, 18, 23, 39, 50, 63, 65, 69, 71, 73, 74, 75, 114, 150, 173, 185

moon, 16, 162
Mordred, 161, 162
Morgana, 161, 162
Morris, 14
Mount Davamand, 59, 219
muscarine, 144
Namarz, 18
Nemrud Dagh, 65, 66, 67
North, 198
Nou Roz, 18
Nurbakhsh, 7, 21, 97, 140, 221
Ocean, 24
Ohrmazd, 53, 57
Ololiuqui, 142, 143
Osiris, 49, 51, 128, 131, 163, 219
OTO, 87, 89, 99, 100, 131, 137
Oxford, 42, 57, 60, 89, 92, 93, 112, 117, 138, 139, 147, 156, 174, 175, 181, 193, 194, 195, 199, 201, 202, 204, 205, 208, 209, 210, 211, 213, 214
Pagan, 195
paganism, 78, 91, 94, 101, 105, 106, 107, 131, 140, 160
Parthian, 28
Peace, 3, 35, 186, 187, 188, 191, 192, 193, 194, 195, 196, 198, 199, 204, 205, 209, 212, 213, 216
Persian, 3, 14, 18, 23, 25, 28, 30, 33, 38, 39, 43, 44, 53, 58, 62, 63, 69, 71, 75, 76, 95, 97, 102, 103, 107, 140, 173, 185, 194
Peyolt, 142, 143

Photosynthesis, 183
Rashnu, 45, 60
right hand, 63, 65, 68, 69, 71, 73, 75, 76, 99, 121, 126, 157, 158
Rosicrucians, 103
Rumi, 102, 202, 214, 215
Sassanian, 30, 32, 95, 96
Scopolamine, 144
Seth, 18, 163
Simurgh, 18, 21
Solstice, 8, 217, 218, 219
Sraosha, 45, 59, 60, 150
star, 21, 159
Sufi, 3, 7, 8, 10, 14, 15, 16, 17, 19, 20, 33, 94, 96, 97, 98, 100, 101, 102, 140, 164, 170, 173, 186, 192, 194, 198, 202, 206, 214, 221
Sun, 8, 18, 21, 38, 48, 51, 69, 73, 218
Taq-e Bostan, 68
Teonaucalt, 142
Thelema, 1, 2, 3, 20, 86
Thelemites, 17, See Thelema
Tishtrya, 45, 55, 218, 219
Urania Lodge, 79, 84
Uther, 161
Vayu, 218, 219
Verethragna, 217, 219
Virgin, 28, 143
warriors, 24

Web, 20, 194, 195, 196, 197, 198, 199, 204, 206, 207, 208, 209, 210, 211, 212, 213

Wicca, 1, 2, 3, 20, 77, 79, 80, 83, 85, 86, 88, 89, 90, 92, 100, 103, 105, 106, 107, 108, 109, 111, 112, 113, 114, 115, 116, 117, 118, 119, 131, 137, 138, 139, 140, 195

Will, 161

Yasht, 24, 38, 39, 52, 55, 57, 58, 59, 69, 150

Yasna, 54, 150

Yew, 14

Zeker, 11, 17, 19, 198

Zeus, 70

Zoroaster, 23, 42, 43, 44, 50, 51, 60

Zoroastrian, 3, 8, 33, 41, 42, 43, 44, 49, 51, 52, 54, 57, 58, 65, 95, 96, 107, 149, 150, 211

Notes:

www.ingramcontent.com/pod-product-compliance
Lightning Source LLC
Chambersburg PA
CBHW031312150426
43191CB00005B/190